KW-358-881

Nov 2010

Preaching Christ in a Postmodern Culture

Preaching Christ in a Postmodern Culture

By

K. A. Beville

CAMBRIDGE
SCHOLARS

P U B L I S H I N G

Preaching Christ in a Postmodern Culture, by K. A. Beville

This book first published 2010

Cambridge Scholars Publishing

12 Back Chapman Street, Newcastle upon Tyne, NE6 2XX, UK

British Library Cataloguing in Publication Data
A catalogue record for this book is available from the British Library

Copyright © 2010 by K. A. Beville

All rights for this book reserved. No part of this book may be reproduced, stored in a retrieval system, or transmitted, in any form or by any means, electronic, mechanical, photocopying, recording or otherwise, without the prior permission of the copyright owner.

ISBN (10): 1-4438-2151-9, ISBN (13): 978-1-4438-2151-3

CONTENTS

PREFACE

I wish to express my sincere thanks to Dr. Michael Haykin, (Professor of Church History and Biblical Spirituality at the Southern Baptist Theological Seminary, Louisville, Kentucky, U.S.A.) for endorsing this work. Gratitude is also expressed here to Rev. Dr. Geoff Pound (Director of Theologians without Borders) for his commendation and helpful advice. These busy men gave of their time generously and graciously and their contribution to promoting this work of research is hereby acknowledged.

I also thank Carol Koulikourdi who liaised with me on behalf of Dr. Andy Nercessian to take me through the particulars of the publishing process for Cambridge Scholar's Publishing. I also wish to express my sincere thanks to Amanda Millar for her professional and patient help in preparing the manuscript in accordance with the required formatting criteria.

Some of the material in *Chapter One: The Shift from Contextualisation to Syncretism* reflects a personal perspective and is not as heavily referenced as the remainder of the work because it was previously published in a number of articles in journals which have a more general readership. Here is the publishing history of these articles: "From Congregations to Audiences" (*The Evangelical Magazine of Wales,* August 2002). "Preaching Christ in a Postmodern Culture" (*Foundations*: *The British Evangelical Council Journal of Theology,* November 2002). "Charming the Church" (*The Banner of Truth Magazine*, May, 2003). "Preaching that Persuades" (*Foundations*: *The British Evangelical Council Journal of Theology,* Spring 2008). The Conclusion includes material, under the sub-heading, "Vox-Pop and Vanishing Pulpits" that was previously published in *The Banner of Truth Magazine*, January 2003.

I refer to preachers as "men" and use the pronoun "he" throughout the work to refer to homileticians. Although I acknowledge that there are denominational and non-denominational churches that have women preachers I do not wish to comment, in this work, on whether or not they have a biblical mandate to do so. Some will argue that Scripture teaches that women are precluded from preaching. Others will contend that the Pauline prohibition to teach men in a church setting was merely a cultural bias and has no warrant in the contemporary context of western society. There are varied and nuanced positions which fall somewhere between these two views. However, the matter is complex and controversial and as such has the potential to change the complexion of this work. In my judgement, therefore, it was better to exclude this issue from the scope of my research.

On a few occasions I refer to the "western church". This merely reflects where my experience is rooted. My travels are making me increasingly conversant with the east and I do not mean to suggest that those outside the west are in any way excluded from this dialogue. Increasing globalisation means that both east and west will continue to influence each other, for bad or good.

This work engages with philosophical and practical theology in order to examine the feasibility of the homiletic task in postmodern culture. Understanding the historical and philosophical development of postmodernism is a necessary prerequisite to proposing an approach to preaching which is cognisant of postmodern sensitivities. I trust I have outlined the origin and evolution of the postmodern psyche with broad brushstrokes. The examination of the expository preaching model and the comparative analysis of deductive and inductive modes of communication suggest a way of moving beyond the apparent impasse. I trust that this will be a clear and useful work for preaching practitioners as well as those involved in training and inspiring those who wish to engage in the challenging task of preaching Christ in a postmodern culture.

Unless otherwise stated, Scripture quotations are from *The Holy Bible*, English Standard Version®, copyright © 2001 by Crossway Bibles, a publishing ministry of Good News Publishers. Used by permission. All rights reserved.

CHAPTER ONE

THE SHIFT FROM CONTEXTUALIZATION TO SYNCRETISM IN THE WESTERN CHRISTIAN CHURCH

i) From congregations to audiences

The following story may help to illustrate the shift from contextualization to syncretism which is taking place in the Christian church in the west. Several years ago a fellow pastor told me that more and more frequently after the Sunday services people came to him and said, "that was good". He had a troubled look on his face and it didn't seem to fit with what he was saying.

"What's your problem?" I probed.

"Well it's nice to be appreciated and to receive some kind of affirmation but these recent comments are not like that" he said.

"If people are helped by the preaching that is surely a positive thing" I suggested.

"Of course" he agreed "but I have often asked, what has helped you?" and the replies indicate that they are not talking about being helped by anything I said but they seem to be commenting on the preaching as a performance!"

"You mean that they are evaluating your style?" I asked incredulously.

"That's exactly right!" he said.

I sympathised with him and exhorted him to keep on preaching. But not long after that the same thing happened to me.

"That was great this morning!" a member of the congregation said with enthusiasm.

"In what way I inquired?"

"Very dramatic" he said confidently.

"How has it helped you?" I asked.

"I enjoyed the passionate delivery" he said.

"And has the message been of any help at all?" I questioned.

The gentleman in question seemed a little affronted and I sensed his embarrassment, it was an awkward moment.

"What you said was good too" he said with a little less enthusiasm. It was evident that he had been commenting only on the method and not the message.

These incidents led me to wonder if some Christian churches have developed a preference for style over content. In themselves they are merely subtle indicators of a more significant shift. Has preaching come to be seen as a public performance that may be evaluated by the same standards of media criticism as one might apply to a stand-up comedian? Is the preacher expected to entertain rather than enlighten? It grieves many who hold a high view of preaching who are mourning the passing of authority that preaching once possessed. The more I thought about it the more I began to see that many churches have unwittingly crossed the line between contextualization and syncretism.

To some extent the question as to where contextualization ends and syncretism begins is debatable. It depends primarily on the emphasis given either to Scripture or cultural setting.[1] Where faithfulness to Scripture is stressed, contextualization is understood as the translation of biblical meanings into contemporary cultural contexts. D. A. Carson says that this model "assigns control to Scripture but cherishes the 'contextualization' rubric because it reminds us that the Bible must be thought about, translated into and preached in categories relevant to the particular cultural context".[2] But, when the cultural context assumes (or is given) priority then that is a different matter. Carson points out that this model "assigns control to the context; the operative term is praxis, which serves as a controlling grid to determine the meaning of Scripture."[3] In this latter situation the purpose is to find what God is already doing in the culture rather than to communicate God's eternal message within the cultural context.

ii) Syncretism

Syncretism occurs when Christian leaders adapt, either consciously or unconsciously, to the prevailing worldviews of their culture. It is the reshaping of Christian beliefs, and practices through cultural accommodation so that they reflect those of the dominant culture. Thus syncretism is the blending of Christian beliefs and practices with those of the dominant culture so that Christianity loses it distinctiveness and speaks with a voice which reflects its culture.[4]

According to Van Rheenan frequently syncretism is birthed from a yearning to make the gospel appear relevant. The church attempts to make its message attractive to outsiders and as these adaptations become regularly assimilated they become an integral part of the church's life. When significant changes in worldview take place within culture, the church then struggles to separate the terrestrial from the celestial. The Christian community, swept along by the ebb and flow of cultural currents, begins to lose her moorings. So syncretism takes place when the church opts into the prevailing cultural assumptions of society.[5]

Under the rubric of modernism, the rationalism of Enlightenment thinking formed an interpretive grid. In any cultural environment the Christian community ought to beware of excessively accommodating itself to the philosophies and practices of the dominant cultures.

There has been a significant paradigm shift best summarised by the word *postmodernism*. Some church people are wandering if it will come into the church. The reality is that it is well embedded in the church and evident in significant shifts in ecclesiology. Many churches have gone beyond the process of contextualizing the gospel in Western culture (which is consumerist and therapeutic) and have married themselves to these core values of society. This kind of syncretism is evident in many ways, especially in the abandonment of traditional modes of communicating truth and a disdain for authority. Douglas Groothuis cautions, "While Christian witness must be savvy concerning the realities of the postmodern condition in order to make the historic Christian message understandable and pertinent to denizens of the contemporary world, this does not mean that we should become postmodernists in the process."[6]

The very architecture of many churches articulates a particular view of preaching. The pulpit is central and elevated because authoritative preaching is central to practice and held in high regard. Thus the furniture speaks eloquently of the theology. Stackhouse has pointed out that, "the public image of the church in general and of individual congregations is very much defined by physical plants. Christians throughout history, therefore, have wisely paid attention to structures that would convey a particular message to the community."[7]

The church is not a building. The church consists of the redeemed people of God and whereas its physical structure make a statement so do its social structures, its connections and interconnections (and indeed the lack of them) in the community.

There are many radical and unnerving developments in how church is practiced today. Much is being advocated as, "living out the gospel *within* its cultural context rather than perpetuating an institutional commitment *apart from* its cultural context".[8] What is called the "attractional church of Chrisendom" is being systematically dismantled in favour of an "incarnational", "missional" model. These buzz words are deceptive because Christians have always endeavoured, by God's grace, to live incarnational lives and tried to keep mission central to the life of the church. Frost and Hirsch readily admit that such a "thoroughgoing recalibration of the church will not always be met with open arms by the prevailing church leadership."[9] This is not surprising as such structures have a history that has evolved over centuries and has served the purpose of the church well during that time. These structures have a theological basis and sacred purpose which were constructed not just in bricks and mortar but with blood, sweat and tears.

Those who want an ecclesiology that devalues and sidelines preaching seem to defend their position with slogans rather than Scripture. People seem to want sound bites rather than sermons. Therapeutic rather than theological messages are sought and self-esteem has been cultivated instead of self-examination in the light of Scripture. There is a shift from theological and expository preaching (which is seen as a tedious, moralising discourse) to therapeutic and empathetic epilogues.

Some congregations are like adolescents who are manifesting the symptoms of vacuity and aimlessness often associated with Attention Deficit Disorder. The word *religion* is seen as an old fashioned term that implies dogma and tradition. The term *spirituality* is more in vogue because it is vague, universal and amorphous and very much in keeping with the postmodern psyche. But the church needs preachers of sound doctrine. It is interesting to note that Scripture identifies all sorts of ungodliness and irreligious attitudes such as adultery, perversion, slave trading, lying and perjury as "contrary to sound doctrine" (1 Timothy 1:10).

Rather than a healthy appetite for what is nutritious there appears to be an insatiable hunger for the frivolous. Has the church become something akin to a fast-food cafeteria where non-nutritious helpings are served up to appease the appetite for fresh stimulation and instant gratification? Many churches are coming under the influence of marketing strategies where congregations are being treated like consumers. Research into their tastes and preferences determine the type of "service" provided. It is easy to observe and decry syncretism in an African or Asian context but harder for us in the West to identify and avoid syncretism in our own situation.

Education was once a means of instilling virtue, training character and upholding the values of citizenship. Now, however, it has capitulated to the individualism and relativism of postmodern culture where self-esteem is the matrix that shapes children's psyches. Curricula have been debased by including misguided and experimental therapeutic programmes in place of the tried and tested, true and trusted.[10] The Christian church seems to be undergoing a similar process.

In many churches today there is a tension between those who see themselves as the *avant-garde* and those who function as the rearguard. Many regard Christian churches as elitist institutions like dusty old museums that function as custodians of tradition. The following analogy may help to illustrate and examine a trend that has parallels in the church today.

Art galleries were once frequented to admire acclaimed works of great art exhibited for the purpose of education and aesthetic stimulation. Today, however, as a result of a desire to be more relevant and popular, by appealing to the masses, many of these galleries have become slaves to novelty. They have forsaken what they deemed to be elitist in the mistaken belief that the space created would allow for the development of greater artistic vitality in their exhibitions. What has actually filled that vacuum is installation "art" often less aesthetic than a municipal landfill site. Furthermore the whole process is driven by notions of success based on profit and numbers. Richard Appignanesi says, "The more experimentation successfully proceeds to diminish the aura and autonomy of art, the more the aura and autonomy become the exclusive properties of exhibitive power – the critical establishment, curators, art-dealers and their clients."[11]

Similarly "progressive" lobbyists in churches advocate changes to appeal to the "un-churched" on the grounds that, such changes will be a catalyst for "growth".[12] Growth is usually narrowly defined as additional numbers of people attending, very few of whom will be new converts. Many of these churches simply attract those similarly disaffected from traditional churches and the haemorrhaging of the latter makes them seem even more anaemic and so the process continues. Because this situation reflects an inherent dissatisfaction with traditional orthopraxy, it is often disgruntled individuals that are striking this keynote for change. Church is too stuffy and elitist, they say, and if it changes, like the art galleries, it will have larger attendance and so on.

In 1997 I attended a summer school on expository and evangelistic preaching in Memphis, Tennessee. This was a very positive experience overall. However, while I was in the USA I had some memorable encounters with different forms of preaching. Surfing the TV channels I came upon "Wrestlers for Jesus". In this programme large, muscular, motor-mouthed men in leotards grappled with each other in a carefully choreographed performance. At the end the victor stepped out of the ring and breathlessly proclaimed, in a voice hoarse from trying to be heard above the cacophonous din of the frenzied audience, "I can do all things through Christ who strengthens me". I wonder if the apologist for this kind of thing would say wrestling is popular and if we want to reach people this is how to do it. At the heart of this argument there is a line of reasoning that sounds strangely familiar.

The most memorable experience I had in the USA was when I visited an Afro-American Church in Tennessee. I was conspicuously Caucasian in the large congregation. It was an unusual service insofar as it was a "Pastor's Appreciation Evening". An electric band began to play. The choir sang and swayed and clapped their hands. They looked very smart in their blue gowns and golden robes. And the congregation danced in the isles or where thy stood at their seats. Then there were a couple of soulful performances by Whitney Houston style soloists. An offering followed this where several large baskets (the kind I keep beside the fire to hold logs!) were distributed. People seemed to give generously. In addition to this some individual gift-wrapped gifts (one being a gentleman's suit), were offered. I was fascinated.

I waited for the preacher with eager expectation and eventually he did arrive. He quoted from Ephesians, "And he gave the apostles, the prophets, the evangelists, the shepherds and teachers." (4:11). After he quoted his text there was a drum roll and a clash of cymbals and this seemed to stimulate the congregation to murmur various responses. He spoke with a rhythm and cadence one might associate with the lyrical style of Martin Luther King; it was a kind of song.[13] There was a drum roll and clash of cymbals after each sentence. The murmur grew louder and responses were exclaimed from every corner of the building. Here, insofar as I can recall, is what he said as he held up his hand.

> My thumb is like the apostles because it touches all the other gifts. My index finger is like the prophets because it points to the problem with people. My longest finger is like the evangelists because it reaches further than the others do. My wedding finger is like the pastor because he is married to the church and my little finger is like the teacher because in this church we don't have a whole lot of that!

This, punctuated with drumming, was the entire sermon. He gathered momentum as he spoke and finished in a crescendo of applause. He spoke only for a few minutes and that included numerous drum rolls! I'm not saying all Afro-American churches are like this but that was my experience. It was a form of entertainment where the *congregation* was more like an *audience*.

The thing that has endured most with me from that experience is the thought that although what he said was memorable it was meaningless. When I hear people saying that preaching should include aids to help people remember the message I think of that occasion. Style can be a distraction from the message or even a substitute in the absence of any real message at all. The advice of Paul to Timothy seems apt, "Until I come, devote yourself to the public reading of Scripture, to exhortation, to teaching." (1 Timothy 4:13).

iii) Charming the church

Some churches have become engaged in experiments to accommodate themselves to the market-driven expectations of the world. The principle seems to be that if the church wants to get its share of the *audience* it must offer them something they want. The church can be popular if it is prepared to trivialise preaching and some think that is a price worth paying. When the congregation of a church is treated like an audience the activity of that church is a vaudeville act rather than a service. Some of these experimental projects have begun modestly with noble motivation but misguided enthusiasm. We now find that such churches have become caricatures; a distortion of what church is meant to be. The emergent church is a postmodern phenomenon that has crossed the boundary between contextualization and syncretism.

This process begins when a church desires to be more acceptable and pleasing to the community. There is, of course, nothing inherently wrong in such a desire but that aspiration may become an unhealthy obsession leading to compromising changes. At first changes made by a church in its practice may seem benign. The church is being mesmerised by entertainment values.

Expository preaching is a form of spiritual discourse that dictates and regulates the content of the communication. The advocates of other forms of ecclesiology that minimise and displace preaching, fail to recognise the inadequacy of alternative methodologies to shape and safeguard the message. At first people are urged to make what may appear to be cosmetic changes and they soon discover that the content of the message is subordinate to its style of presentation. This is part of a dumbing-down process where optional means of transmitting the message are advocated. Paul's instruction to the Roman church needs to be restated in today's hedonistic society, "Do not be conformed to this world, but be transformed by the renewal of your mind, that by testing you may discern what is the will of God, what is good and acceptable and perfect." (Romans12:2).

Preaching produces serious-minded and biblically informed people whereas in its absence there is shallowness. Preaching is seen, in some circles, as no more than a cultural bias. But in an age of epistemological relativism preaching as a means of prophetic proclamation has a healthy influence on churches where it is central to its life.[14]

There has been an epistemological shift that is reflected in eclectic approaches to communicating truth. However, authoritative preaching makes demands on its hearers and one is never left merely impressed with the eloquence of the preacher. A sermon is more than semantics. The hearer is made aware of the clear implications of the message. Ultimately it is not the sensuous experience of the preaching or the superior logic of the argument but the power of the Holy Spirit that is at work. It is a cognitive communication and an emotional experience but primarily it is a spiritual awakening and quickening of the soul. In other words, preaching is not just rhetoric it has a spiritual resonance that vibrates in the soul. It trains believers to tutor their minds and integrate experience in a process that shapes identity by defining and regulating understanding of the truth in accordance with biblical patterns. But it requires in the hearer a residual faith in the authenticity and authority of the message as well as the medium of communication.

I grew up in Limerick City, in Ireland, where the river Shannon was a dominant feature of the geographical landscape as well as the recreational and occupational life of the people. In my lifetime that great waterway has been slowly polluted and it is no longer suitable for bathing. It is amazing what can be lost in a generation.

The church is like a river insofar as changes in its life are sometimes gradual and imperceptible at first. Like the river it can be slowly polluted. It takes time before the river becomes so poisonous that the fish die. Yet the river looks the same as before and one could still take a boat ride on it. In other words even when life has been taken from it the river does not disappear, nor do all of its uses but its value has been diminished and its degraded condition will have harmful effects throughout the landscape.

Boating is now a leisure activity on the Shannon but in a previous generation life was sustained by the fish caught in that great waterway. The river is still there but it's not what it used to be and it is not what it appears to be! So it is with the church that is being slowly polluted. If a church merely has a recreational function in the life of the community it has ceased to be what it ought to be.

In some churches an ephemeral and experiential enterprise masquerading as preaching has replaced the traditional sermon. The transcendent has been displaced by the trivial.

Preaching is not meant to be inert. It is not merely about imparting information. There has to be an information-action ratio where relevant information is generated into action, otherwise the information is no more than an abundance of irrelevant facts, although in any communication environment input will always exceed output. In other words what one is informed about will always exceed the possibility of action based on that information. The question is; what exactly should that ratio be?

Detractors of preaching will say that the congregations are faced with the problem of an information glut, which is another way of saying that there is diminished spiritual potency. They might suggest that the Sunday evening sermons dislodge the Sunday morning sermons from the minds of hearers. Surely, if this is true it is not less information that is needed but more action.

Some might say that preaching gives answers to questions not asked in postmodern culture. This criticism does not take account of the fact that preaching is dialogical and helps hearers ask the right questions.

It no longer seems strange now to have church events where there is no preaching, take, for example what is sometimes called "low-key evangelism". Various activities can be arranged in the church building with the purpose in mind to "just get people across the threshold" and into a "non-threatening environment". This has come to seem natural rather than bizarre. The fact that many have lost the sense that this is strange is an indication of their desire to be inoffensive. The desire to be accepted and the need to appear relevant may turn the church in a wrong direction. Remember the words of Paul, "For the word of the cross is folly to those who are perishing, but to us who are being saved it is the power of God." (1 Corinthians 1:18).

Is preaching disappearing? It has certainly moved to the periphery and other things are beginning to take its place at the centre. The demise of preaching is part of a wider issue, namely, the crisis of confidence in biblical wisdom, its authority, sufficiency and efficacy. The writer to the Hebrews should put our view of God's Word in perspective, "For the word of God is living and active, sharper than any two-edged sword, piercing to the division of soul and of spirit, of joints and of marrow, and discerning the thoughts and intentions of the hear.t" (Hebrews 4:12).

Many churches are reaching the point where methodology is displacing theology as the area of competence over which a pastor must have expert control? Paul told the church in Rome that "faith comes from hearing, and hearing through the word of Christ" (Romans 10: 17). There is a message that must be told in a method ordained by God for that purpose. Paul's instruction to Timothy applies to today and has not been rescinded, "preach the word; be ready in season and out of season." (2 Timothy 4:2).

iv) Developing a new approach to preaching

We live in a postmodern society where the very concept of objective, absolute truth is perceived not just as antiquated but absurd. Epistemological and ethical fragmentation has led to moral relativism. The search for an apologetic strategy in postmodern society is a formidable challenge for the Christian church. Is it possible to find a biblically informed and effective contemporary approach? Is the apologetic task feasible in a culture that denies the existence of objective, universal truth? The biblical instruction is clear, 'always being prepared to make a defence to anyone who asks you for a reason for the hope that is in you; yet do it with gentleness and respect' (1 Peter 3:15).

Under the auspices of modernity colonialism and capitalism flourished and in the twentieth- century, Nazism gained a stranglehold on Europe and Marxist social experiments quarantined millions from what it perceived as the evils of free market economics.[15] Modernity failed to create the utopia to which it aspired and these ideologies came to be seen as oppressive metanarratives. Christianity has also come to be viewed in this way.

There has been a significant shift in thinking which has relevance to those engaged in preaching. With the modernist mindset if something could be proved as true, or at least reasonable, the logical conclusion was that it ought to be accepted. The modernist who accepted the veracity of the Christian message was being hypocritical in not accepting its personal implications. But the postmodernist is not constrained in this way. He is free to acknowledge its truth but not necessarily accept it because he lives in a relativistic world.

Under the modernist rubric preaching was a linear mode of discourse, which was generally coherent, sequential and essentially logical. The expository sermon, therefore, used arguments, hypotheses, reasons and refutations as traditional instruments of rational discourse. As such it cultivated inferential thinking. In the context of postmodernism one might ask what place has a style of communication, which has a propositional content that appeals for understanding as a prerequisite to faith? It not only assumes and requires in the hearer an aptitude to organise information systematically and methodically but inferentially. But the postmodern mind works differently and a new approach is needed.

Modernist preaching was essentially an intelligent activity that assumed cognitive skills amongst hearers. The modernist sermon had a particular line of thought where judgements and application were made in a coherent and orderly argument. It is not that it was essentially intellectual but that it was inherently rational. In other words it assumed that reason would be employed to enlighten. Even though people could be moved emotionally by preaching they were required firstly to understand its content and accept its conclusions.

Preaching was, after all, expositing a text that has syntactical structure and content that can be explicated. There was, therefore, not just a faith in the truth of the text but a concomitant and coterminous faith in reason itself. Thus preaching engaged the intellect. It assumed that people are rational and analytical creatures. Preaching in the Enlightenment period focused on conveying biblical information and making claims in propositional form.

Thus preaching constructed a context in which the question: "is this true or false?" was relevant and meaningful. Whether it was sophisticated or simple it appealed to cognitive powers based on understanding and reason. It had a bias towards the ability to think conceptually, deductively and sequentially and because it was based on reason and order it had an inherent aversion for contradiction. It was never about merely knowing facts, even biblical facts. It involved an understanding of the implications, historical background and logical and theological connections.

But in the postmodern world reality has been dismembered, meanings have been wrenched out of logical contexts and life has become idiosyncratic. The postmodern mind has a predisposed antipathy to preaching because it understands it to be authoritarian, absolutist and oppressive. Logic, reason, sequential thought and rules of contradiction are abandoned. In aesthetics this is evident in Dadaism, the movement that flourished primarily in Switzerland, Germany and France from 1916 to 1920. In this cult aesthetic philosophy principles and practice in the arts, especially painting, were based on intentional irrationality, cynicism, anarchy and negation of the laws of beauty and social organisation. Dadaism has wider geographical, chronological and philosophical resonance as evidenced in today's postmodern psyche.

Thus it does not seem to matter that some 'truths' in the postmodern world actually contradict each other. How can this be explained? Contradiction requires mutually exclusive assertions that cannot possibly both, in the same context, be true. It is context, therefore, that defines contradiction. If somebody says he prefers grapes to peaches and in the same breath says that he prefers peaches to grapes there is not, necessarily, a contradiction if one statement is made in the context of choosing a motif in curtain or wallpaper patterns and the other expresses his eating preference. But if these statements are made in a singular context, say, in relation to decor alone, they are contradictory. Without a continuous and coherent context there is no such thing as contradiction.

Therefore when preaching the gospel is taken out of the context of linear history and presented in a world of discontinuity and fragmentation it is "a truth" that does not contradict "other truths". The Bible, for example, presents a certain degree of Palestinian history. It has one continuous and coherent perspective. In today's world it is just one version of truth where contradictory perspectives have equal validity because culture is seen as the defining context.

To what extent, therefore, if any, should either the message or methodology be adapted to accommodate postmoderns? How can an apologetic strategy be shaped that is relevant in the context of postmodernity and uncompromising in its eternal message? What are the challenges that such strategies present in the context of the local church in relation to preaching?

Individualism and relativism are features of our postmodern society. It is not unlike the situation that prevailed in Israel at the time of the Judges, before the authority of the king emerged, "In those days there was no king in Israel. Everyone did what was right in his own eyes." (Judges 21:25). If individualism and relativism are features of contemporary culture then there is a great need for the church to counter this by being incarnational and transforming communities. In a society where rational discourse has failed Christians ought to manifest the reality of the power of God in radically altered lives through intentional missional activity.

Nevertheless there is a danger that, in attempting to shape an effective apologetic strategy in a postmodern society, pragmatism will gain the ascendancy and secularise the church. It may be timely to take heed to the warning of Paul to the Galatian Church, "See to it that no one takes you captive by philosophy and empty deceit, according to human tradition, according to the elemental spirits of the world, and not according to Christ." (Colossians 2:8).

Increasingly churches are being influenced by postmodernity. Some are becoming theologically foggy and non-doctrinal with an all-inclusive ecclesiology. In such churches there is an appeal to feelings that puts emotionalism at the centre of practice and this affects preaching. This is evident in a shift of emphasis from truth to technique where psychology tends to eclipse Christology.

The church must not capitulate to postmodernism but it has a duty to engage with it for the sake of the gospel. Thus it needs to be seeker-sensitive but not seeker-centred. The desire to be relevant must be subordinate to the obligation to be faithful. Where the desire to be relevant is uppermost unpalatable truths are sidelined as "unhelpful". In such circumstances there is an admission that these truths are unmarketable. Contemporary culture is individualistic and hedonistic and this is reflected in elements of the church which are pleasure-seeking, experiential-focused and Christian-centred rather than communal, sacrificial and Christ-centred.

There is an obligation to continue to engage in proclamation and not merely silently model Christlikeness through mission activity which is non-proclamatory and engages in development work. That would be a contradiction because Christ engaged in proclamation. It should not be a case of either one or the other but rather both together. The Word of God should not be dismissed as irrelevant in a postmodern society because Scripture says that God's Word will never be void of power:

> For as the rain and the snow come down from heaven and do not return there but water the earth, making it bring forth and sprout, giving seed to the sower and bread to the eater, so shall my word be that goes out from my mouth; it shall not return to me empty, but it shall accomplish that which I purpose, and shall succeed in the thing for which I sent it. (Isaiah 55:10-11).

It is important that Christians are informed about the mindset of people today. It is interesting to note that in the list of people who came to join the Old Testament King David in battle at a crucial juncture in the history of Israel there were, "men who had understanding of the times." (1 Chronicles 12:32). Such people (men and women) are needed today at an equally crucial juncture in the history of God's people.

In a conversation between Jesus and the Roman Procurator of Judea, Pontius Pilate, Jesus said, "For this purpose I was born and for this purpose I have come into the world-to bear witness to the truth." (John 18:37). Then Pilate asked, "What is truth?" (John 18:38). The Enlightenment project was, ostensibly at least, a search for truth but that is now deemed to be a failed project. In the postmodern context nobody is asking; "what is truth?" because the search for absolute truth has been abandoned. Jesus said, "I am the way, and the truth, and the life. No one comes to the Father except through me." (John 14:6). Peter proclaimed; "there is salvation in no one else, for there is no other name under heaven given among men by which we must be saved." (Acts 4:12). These words are as politically incorrect now as they were in the first century when they were uttered. They may engender the same kind of hostility in today's postmodern world as they did then. In seeking to find an apologetic strategy that is contemporary the church must be unapologetic about preaching Christ.

Preaching the cross will always be seen by many as an "oppressive meta-narrative" because of its universal application. It warns of an ultimate judgement, whether that is understood as exclusion from the eschatological kingdom or eternal conscious torment in hell for those who do not repent is a moot point. But it is a reckoning based on "truth". Scripture says, "the judgment of God is according to truth." (Romans 2:2 NKJV). In spite of postmodern assertions to the contrary there is an ultimate standard, or to put it another way, there is absolute truth.

The glory of the gospel is that it offers salvation to all that trust in the work of Christ. But to the postmodern mind preaching may be merely discredited rhetoric and the challenge is to find a way of preaching that connects with postmoderns.

How Christians live in contemporary culture is crucial. The Old Testament character Daniel, for example, found himself to be an alien, a displaced person, in Babylon. But he made a conscious decision that he would not be overwhelmed by the culture of his day. That is what Nebuchadnezzar was trying to do. He was trying to spiritually subjugate God's people so that they would lose their unique identity and become like everybody else. Scripture says, "But Daniel resolved that he would not defile himself with the king's food, or with the wine that he drank. Therefore he asked the chief of the eunuchs to allow him not to defile himself." (Daniel 1:8). Believers, too, must make a conscious decision not to allow the prevailing culture to swallow them.

When John the Baptist was imprisoned and began to doubt that Jesus was the Messiah he sent two messengers to Jesus to inquire if he was really the Christ. It is interesting to see how Jesus replied. He said, "And he answered them, 'Go and tell John what you have seen and heard: the blind receive their sight, the lame walk, lepers are cleansed, and the deaf hear, the dead are raised up, the poor have good news preached to them.'" (Luke 7:22). John doubted the deity of Jesus and doubted all that he had preached in heralding the Christ. Jesus does not answer him merely with words of reassurance. He does not give a theological dissertation on the fulfilment of prophecy in the person and work of Christ. Rather, he asks the messengers to report on what they have witnessed of the transforming power of God as demonstrated in his miracles. His activity authenticated his authority. To those like John the Baptist who doubt and despair the church must be messengers from the Saviour who talk as first hand witnesses of the transforming power of Christ so that they may say with John the apostle:

> That which was from the beginning, which we have heard, which we have seen with our eyes, which we looked upon and have touched with our hands, concerning the word of life...we proclaim also to you, so that you too may have fellowship with us; and indeed our fellowship is with the Father and with his Son Jesus Christ. (1 John 1:1-4).

This is important in a postmodern culture where winning arguments is not so much impossible as irrelevant. The gospel is not just about words of persuasion but also about pointing to evidence of that transforming power and being evidence of that power.

Many people in postmodern society are deaf, blind, dumb and diseased with sin ("sin", of course, is a politically incorrect word). But postmodern society, in spiritual terms, is lame and lost. The church has a transforming vision to transmit but if it just talks about how things could be it is falling short. For example, Christians cannot just talk about love but must live it. When reason and rational argument fail (as they do in postmodern culture) relationship may fill the vacuum.

Some sections of the Christian church could do more to show the relevance of faith to society. Some have narrowly defined "mission" as evangelism and rejected what it sees as the "social gospel" because it understands mission as, a more purely "spiritual" activity. The polemical debate has polarised the Christian community. Many people today are interested in environmental issues. The Christian can show that the ultimate ecological ethic is rooted in the creator. The church is failing society by leaving issues such as these in the hands of new age, secular activists.

The concept of *missio Dei* (mission of God) needs to be universally adapted by all sections of the Christian church. The term refers to the Christian theological understanding of mission where missionary theory and practice is founded in the missionary activity of the Triune God.[16] David Bosch states it thus, "The classical doctrine of the *missio Dei* as God the Father sending the Son, and God the Father and the Son sending the Spirit was expanded to include yet another 'movement': Father, Son and Holy Spirit sending the church into the world."[17] So this serves as the *raison d'être* and impetus for mission. It continues to function as a corrective to the notion of mission as merely "evangelism" and gives a unifying theological theme to mission activity. It has been well said by Pachuau, "It is not the church that has a mission, it is God's mission that has a church."[18]

It is perfectly reasonable to examine different ways of communicating (other than preaching) with contemporary culture. However, the church must be careful not to yield to the temptation to market itself to "unchurched" consumers by appealing to their emotions and forsaking the duty to teach people to think biblically. The first strand in an apologetic strategy will be to preach the Word of God. The second will be community relationships. Christians are messengers, with a message but they are also models. One of the aims of preaching to congregations is to enable people to model the message.

Starting with some observations relating to shifts in ecclesiology and identifying them as a move beyond contextualization to syncretism the subsequent chapters in this discussion go on to assess the feasibility of preaching in a postmodern culture which rejects both the idea of absolute truth and authority used as power. The broad contours of the historical and philosophical development of postmodernism will be traced. In the contemporary epistemological context the Enlightenment project is generally deemed to have failed and Christianity is perceived by many as an oppressive metanarrative. The rational experiment which spanned the period 1789 to 1989 has not succeeded in leading to the paradise it promised. In a world that is becoming increasingly sceptical and cynical and where preaching practitioners are becoming more and more disillusioned, the search for insight and guidelines about preaching to postmoderns becomes imperative. In a relational age, the old supremacy of rationality is impotent and it is important to distinguish between *authoritarian* and *authoritative* preaching; the latter allowing hope for the survival of the homiletic task. Humility is preferable to certitude and persuasion must be redefined to include *logos* (the inherent logic of the message itself), *ethos* (the integrity of the speaker) and *pathos* (the emotions evoked by the oration).

What is needed is an approach to preaching which is cognizant of postmodern culture. This may be achieved by evaluating the merits and demerits of deductive and inductive modes of communication where the preacher is understood as one who facilitates a dynamic encounter with the living God. An inductive approach to expository preaching, along with employing narrative, seems to be the most powerful and effective means of engaging the minds, emotions and wills of postmodern listeners. This approach signposts a way forward in the labyrinthine complexity of the new paradigm and demonstrates that the homiletic task is still feasible in a new epistemological, ontological and ethical context.

Certain *a priori* assumptions govern assessment of the various theological attempts to reconstruct and communicate ideas of truth and revelation in the light of the postmodern challenge. Consequently, all theologies that contravene these *a priori* assumptions (by showing themselves to be, self-contradictory, self-enclosed, self-referential and without ethical significance) are rejected. These assumptions are grounded ultimately in the belief that God, by his very nature, never contradicts himself and that he is concerned about ethical matters. I suggest that these assumptions are reasonable. These criteria have informed the discussion on three levels, determined by the nature of the postmodern challenge. Postmodernism challenges all theologies of truth and revelation, in the area of epistemology, ontology and morality.

With regard to the ontological challenge ideas of revelation and truth have to take into account the fact that the method of deconstruction has fundamentally altered classical world-views. This alteration is twofold. Firstly, with regard to language there is the deconstruction of the referential nature of language. Secondly, there is the deconstruction of the Cartesian *cogito*.

Theologies of truth and revelation must neither be conceived to be dominating and oppressive nor completely frivolous and unperturbed by ethical questions. Relativity may never be sought to be overcome by demands for unconditional obedience, based on so-called indubitable divine revelation, formulated in fixed and timeless propositions. Neither may relativity lapse into a complete relativism which rests in the radical incommensurability of different discourses. This position relinquishes the quest to bring about a more ethical and harmonious society.

CHAPTER TWO

UNDERSTANDING POSTMODERNISM: ISSUES PERTAINING TO THE FEASIBILITY OF THE HOMILETIC TASK IN THE CONTEMPORARY EPISTEMOLOGICAL CONTEXT

Much has been written in recent decades describing the phenomenon of postmodernism. What is postmodernism? What are its essential features? For example, Walter Truett Anderson in his book, *Reality Isn't What it Used to Be*, says that the world has been radically altered, "In recent decades we have passed, like Alice slipping through the looking glass, into a New World."[1]

He suggests that this altered state of consciousness is the New World of postmodernism.

There is no consensus view of what postmodernism is, although key features of this phenomenon may be identified. Postmodernism defines itself according to what it is not: modern. But in what sense is it "post"? Any or all of the meanings: *result, aftermath, afterbirth, development, denial,* or *rejection* of modernism presents a case. Perhaps it is some combination of these meanings.[2]

It is not clear exactly what it is, because it resists and obscures the sense of modernism. Its name suggests, in a literal sense, that it is a new age which has surpassed the age of modernism. Any age is identified and defined by evidence of historic changes in the way people see, think and produce. Such changes relate primarily to art, theory and economic history. It is obvious that changes have taken place in these spheres.

The word postmodern is part of the academic parlance of today. It is part of the vocabulary of literary criticism and more general communication.[3] However it is not at all clear precisely what the term means. Daniel J. Adams says that there are, "Few terms as commonly used, and just as commonly misunderstood as postmodernism."[4] For some, such as Lawrence Cahoone, postmodernism represents "the defeat of modern European theology, metaphysics, authoritarianism, colonialism, racism, and domination."[5] For others, postmodernism is a radical intellectual movement intent on subverting civilisation.[6] Postmodernism has even been described as "a goofy collection of hermetically obscure writers who are really talking about nothing at all."[7]

Charles Colson is a writer who represents a particular strand of opinion that offers a bleak picture of postmodernism. He claims:

> Today, all the major ideological constructions are being tossed on the ash heap of history. All that remains is the cynicism of postmodernism, with its false assertions that there is no objective truth or meaning, that we are free to create our own truth as long as we understand that it's nothing more than an illusion.[8]

Is this an accurate portrayal of postmodernism? Alister McGrath is correct in his statement that "a full definition of postmodernism is virtually impossible."[9] Cahoone suggests that it is a "mistake to seek a single essential meaning" of postmodernism that is "applicable to all the term's instances."[10]

Postmodernism is a problematic concept to clarify primarily because the concepts associated with it are complex. It is not a monolithic ideology. For example, there are several postmodern perspectives in art (including film and music), architecture and so on.[11] David Ray Griffin indicates that there are various postmodern theologies.[12] The term postmodernism also pertains to some of the principal cultural and intellectual movements such as feminism, pragmatism, existentialism, deconstruction, and post-empiricist philosophy of science.[13] Postmodernism is not easy to define: it is like looking at the negative of a film and trying to see the image represented. It is associated more with what it rejects than with what it positively affirms.[14] For Adams, postmodernism is a concept "that has not yet discovered how to define itself in terms of what is, but only in terms of what it has just-now-ceased to be."[15]

In addition, the attempt to clarify the concept of postmodernism is further complicated by lack of consensus amongst authors about how it ought to be defined.[16] Postmodernism has been classified in manifold ways: as an era, a condition, a state of mind or attitude, and a philosophical movement.[17] As Griffin points out, postmodernism "is used in a confusing variety of ways, some of them contradictory to others."[18] Furthermore, efforts to define postmodernism are considered by some of its adherents as an inimical desire to pigeonhole a concept that is inherently amorphous.[19] It is not always easy to clarify where modernism ends and postmodernism begins.[20] There is even no agreement about when postmodernism began or when the term was first used.

Cahoone credits Rudolf Pannwitz as the first to use the designation in 1917. Pannwitz's usage delineates the nihilism of modern man as outlined by Friedrich Nietzsche.[21] Others credit Frederico de Oniz with initiating the term *postmodernismo* in 1934. Carl F. H. Henry says that John Cobb first coined the word, as it is currently understood, in 1964.[22] However, it must be said that postmodernism is generally understood to be a philosophical word that refers to a movement that started in France in the 1960s and continued to be cultivated in the United States.[23]

Notwithstanding the difficulties of defining postmodernism, some working definition is necessary. It can be said with certainty that postmodernism refers to the period "after the modern world."[24] McGrath says it is the "general intellectual outlook arising after the collapse of modernism."[25] It is a reaction to the modernism of Western civilisation.[26] It is a counter-culture worldview that is inherently antithetical to the Enlightenment's confidence in universal rational principles.[27] As postmodern doctrine is generally taken to be true in Western culture, it is apt to refer to the present time as the postmodern era.[28] Ronald J. Allen says that:

> While postmodernism is an extremely diverse phenomenon, people who identify themselves as postmodern typically eschew understandings of the world that are universal (totalizing), assert relativity in every form of awareness, seek to expose and critique privilege, and celebrate particularity, diversity and pluralism in all life forms.[29]

Postmodernism is an influential worldview. "Postmodernism is a new set of assumptions about reality", Dockery asserts.[30] "It impacts our literature, our dress, our art, our architecture, our music, our sense of right and wrong, our self-identity, and our theology."[31]

As postmodernism is a reaction to modernism, a basic knowledge of modernism and pre-modernism is helpful for acquiring an understanding of postmodernism. As Millard J. Erickson states, "If we would understand postmodernism, then, we must first understand the two periods that preceded it, namely, the pre-modern and the modern."[32]

i) Pre-modernism as precursor and progenitor of modernism

Postmodernism's more remote predecessor, the pre-modern period, is generally thought to refer to the pre-Enlightenment era incorporating the ancient and medieval periods.[33] What are the essential features of this epoch? Erickson says the pre-modern world was characterised by "belief in the rationality of the universe."[34] In the pre-modern period, reality was understood as an organic, organised and inter-related entity. Furthermore it was perceived as dualistic.

Not only was there the immediately identifiable natural world but there was also the less obvious, though nonetheless real, supernatural domain. If God created and sustained the universe then everything had a pattern and a purpose. This dualistic rationality and spiritual order therefore permitted humanity a privileged place in the hierarchical structure. Stanley J. Grenz notes, "God stood at the apex, followed by the angelic hosts; humans found their place 'a little lower than the heavenly beings' (Psalm 8:5) but above the rest of the created order."[35]

Phenomena in the pre-modern world were perceived and explained by the purpose they served in teleological terms.[36] In theological terms, that is the doctrine of design and purpose in the material world. In other words, the pre-modern mind thought of the world as a reality designed by God for a particular purpose. This is particularly true in the Western world, where the great architect of the universe was thought to be the sovereign God superintending the affairs of history to the ultimate fulfilment of his will. This, incidentally, is by no means a discarded way of thinking in the church today. Indeed many adherents of the three major monotheistic Abrahamic religions (Judaism, Christianity and Islam) share this way of thinking. History was seen as a linear process moving inexorably toward an ultimate climax. Henry notes that the pre-modern age "held that nature and history reflect God's immutable ordering of the cosmos. Its worldview elaborated a distinctive understanding of the nature and destiny of the human self in a meaningful and purposive universe created and ruled by God."[37] Another essential feature of the pre-modern period was a fundamental realism that believed in the objective existence of the world.[38] The world was seen as actually existing in a manner external to the mind or independently from anyone's perception of it.

The pre-modern period held to a correspondence theory of truth. Assertions were thereby deemed to be true if they accurately stated the characteristics of the real nature of what they sought to describe. The converse was also held to be true, and so statements that did not accurately describe reality were understood to be false.[39] Ronald J. Allen says that, "The modern preacher attempted to offer an understanding of Christian faith that was consistent with Enlightenment presuppositions concerning truth."[40]

ii) Modernism as precursor and progenitor of postmodernism

In order to fully understand how the cultural shift from modernism to postmodernism has taken place, it is important to clarify what is meant by the modern age. We have suggested that the modern age lasted two-hundred years (1789-1989).[41] But it was also noted that others argue for an earlier date for the beginning of the modern period, going back to René Descartes in 1641 when he promulgated the famous statement, *cogito ergo sum*, "I think, therefore I am."[42] It is important to trace the historical and philosophical developments which have led to the emergence of postmoderns. Descartes heralded the beginning of a whole new movement in philosophy. Rationalism burst onto the scene and gave epistemology a new framework for answering the questions: "what can be known?" and "how can it be known that anything is known?" Descartes' rationalism sought epistemological answers through doubting everything. He resolved as a first principle, "never to accept anything for true which he did not clearly know to be such."[43] Cartesian doubt, and the rationalism that it spawned, opened the door for the scientific method and suggested a whole new way of explaining all of reality.[44]

The Enlightenment was in part a reaction to the premodern preoccupation with superstition, supernatural speculation and revelation. It is important at this point to say that fundamental philosophical changes occurred in the area of epistemology which predated and predetermined the socio-cultural shift. These new insights supported the view that reality could be explained in ways that excluded the necessity for believing in a supernatural being in control of reality. While a positive development for science, for religion, rationalism was threatening to explain away any need for God at all.[45]

The rationalism of Descartes opened the door for scientific investigation and the whole array of scientific enquiry gave a new sense of hope to a world that had been locked into a worldview that explained reality with premodern superstitions and supernatural speculation. Some were even heralding science as having replaced religion as a source of absolute truth. Graham Johnston says, "People no longer needed to cling to superstitions or even biblical revelation because now, through empirical study and scientific rationalism one could conclusively determine what was true and real."[46]

iii) Empiricism

Empiricism is a branch of philosophy based on observation, experience, or experiment rather than on theory. Descartes promulgated his philosophy in the 1600s, but a new epistemological system, *Empiricism*, emerged in the eighteenth century. The Empiricists, including John Locke (1632-1704), George Berkeley (1685-1753) and David Hume (1711-1766), were not content to reason strictly on the basis of so-called self-evident truths. Instead they sought answers to the problem of knowledge through experience, especially the senses. Although David Hume is included among the Empiricists, he is best known as a sceptic. In his brand of empiricism, he doubted that anything can be known for sure. In fact, he advanced the idea that one cannot prove the existence of anything outside oneself.[47]

iv) Scepticism

Scepticism is an area of philosophy that questions the possibility of knowledge. This movement through the history of philosophy from Rationalism, through to Empiricism to modern Scepticism demonstrates the pathway that postmodernism has taken to arrive at the culture of today. Rationalism replaced revelation by suggesting that reason is on a higher order of knowing than accepting what to some may have seemed like superstition. Rationalism purported that reason alone is sufficient to discover truth, while Empiricism held that all knowledge proceeds from sense perception.[48] Modern scepticism is not so much a philosophical period, as it is a method for doing epistemology.[49] Polluck and Cruz point out that, "Historically, philosophers have often motivated the simple epistemic tasks with the help of sceptical arguments."[50] Even Descartes began his reasoning by doubting. Much of what philosophers have done in the past has been motivated in some way to answer the sceptic. Postmodernism appears to have drawn much of its thinking from the wells of scepticism that have been dug in each period of philosophical development.[51]

v) Romanticism

Some people became dissatisfied with the mechanistic view of reality which was a feature of the Enlightenment. Thus Romanticism emerged countering the Enlightenment assumption that reason is the most important faculty, with the assumption that emotion is the essence of humanness.[52]

Romantics encouraged the idea of getting in touch with the inner self; that lives only have meaning in the inner world of emotions. They criticised civilisation as a force that enslaves. They gloried in the past and sought to bring humanity back to nature away from technology and materialism.

Their view of nature in harmony however, was completely refuted by Darwin's theory of evolution. Darwin set out to prove that nature is actually violent and argued that species survived and adapted through what he called, "the survival of the fittest". Romanticism was never able to prevail and finally disappeared in the latter nineteenth-century, "before the hard-edged certainties of neo-Enlightenment materialism".[53]

vi) Existentialism

The materialism that emerged did not provide the kind of hope and satisfaction that people craved. In response Existentialism emerged as a new worldview that offered meaning to individuals even in the light of the assertions of materialism.[54] Existentialism is the philosophical theory emphasising the existence of the individual as a free and self-determining agent. This new worldview, although accepting that there is no inherent meaning in life, asserted that life can be made meaningful by making choices. Søren Kierkegaard (1813-1855) argued that, "what matters is the subjective choice, the leap of faith, one's commitment to the absurd".[55] Veith asserts that, "romanticism and existentialism paved the way for today's postmodern worldview".[56]

Existentialism makes little sense without understanding something of the major shift that occurred through Kant and Hegel. Immanuel Kant (1724-1804) represents the "climax of eighteenth-century rationalism and empiricism." Kant asserted that, "the mind does not actually perceive things as they are in themselves."[57] He contended that things are perceived as they appear to the senses but the thing itself, in its essence cannot be known.[58] In other words, there is a great divide between what is perceived; the "phenomenal" and the object actually being perceived; the "noumenal". Kant was trying to formulate a way of countering the scepticism of Hume, but what he did in fact was create even greater difficulties for everyone who followed after him.[59]

The optimism of the Enlightenment period was all but gone by Kant's time. During the golden period of the Enlightenment, there was a sense that humanity had finally come to the place where it could be said that one can know something for sure. There was a future goal of finding a sort of unified field theory for philosophy, some circle within which all that is known could be categorised. This goal was also shaping science.

Physicists were searching for the unified field theory that would unite electricity, magnetism, gravity and every other "field" occurring in nature. Philosophers wanted the same thing, but Kant intervened in this ideal by creating a huge gap between what is perceived and what can be known for sure.

vii) Hegel

Friedrich Hegel (1770-1831) attempted to bridge the gap with his concept of "synthesis".[60] What Hegel formulated, borrowing from Kant's ideas, was a revolutionary concept. Instead of beginning with antithesis or Cartesian doubt, he asserted, "let us think in terms of thesis-antithesis, with the answer always being synthesis."[61] That has implications for the pursuit of knowledge, suggesting that all truth is relative. Instead of living with concepts of "either this or that" this hypothesis suggests ways to say, "both this *and* that".

Schaeffer calls this period in philosophical development, "the line of despair".[62] By using the word "despair" he is not suggesting that there is no hope for the philosopher or for humanity, but there is a sense of despair over ever being able to bridge Kant's phenomenal-noumenal gap. There is despair that one may never be sure of knowing anything. In short there can be no certainty of the possibility of going beyond surface depth. Up to this point philosophers were optimistic, but after Kant and Hegel, there was a move to try to pick up the pieces and move on. Kierkegaard tries to help the project, offering the chance to bridge Kant's nuomenal and phenomenal gap by a leap of faith. He argued that it is possible to have an experience that will validate existence and give some meaning to life. With the synthesis of Hegel still lying on the surface of the philosophical landscape, however, all that could be hoped for was some sort of relative truth. Even after Kierkegaard's attempt to leap the, "broad, ugly ditch", philosophers were still concluding that nothing can be known for sure.

In the postmodern period there is a shift toward denial of objective reality and the rejection of any possibility of absolute truth. Alvin Plantinga summarises postmodern repudiation of modernism by noting the rejection of classical foundationalism, the correspondence theory of truth, a representational theory of language, objectivity of thought and belief, and inclusive theories of reality or "metanarratives".[63] These "modern" views, which postmodernists reject, are representative of the various intervals of optimism toward the pursuit of truth and objectivity in the modern period.

The modern era has both comparisons and contrasts with the pre-modern period. One of the striking contrasts between the pre-modern and modern worlds is that the modern world was essentially humanistic. Humanism, as the name suggests, puts man at the centre of reality rather than God. In spite of the fact that many people believed in God, the deity was not viewed as the starting point for understanding the universe. Henry suggests that the modern world "transferred to itself the attributes that had long characterised the traditional deity."[64]

The philosophy of René Descartes made a significant contribution to this development and he is rightly understood (by many) as the founder of modernism. He declared the cognitive domain of the human mind's conviction of its own existence as the place where understanding reality began. Thus, as already noted, there was a significant shift of emphasis from God to man.[65] As Richard Tarnas explains, "In effect, Descartes unintentionally began a theological Copernican revolution, for his mode of reasoning suggested that God's existence was established by human reason and not vice versa."[66]

The modern period was also naturalistic. Some scientists practised "doxological science" where their work was performed to the glory of God. But most intellectuals "gravitated toward naturalistic explanations of everything."[67] The universe was viewed as a self-contained unit and reality was restricted to it alone.[68]

One of the essential features of the modern period was its central belief in the power of human reason.[69] They believed that human reason could lead to an objective understanding of knowledge and reality. This view is encapsulated in John Locke's statement "*Reason* must be our last judge and guide in everything."[70] Thus modern Christian apologists, for example, attempted to offer an understanding of faith that was consistent with Enlightenment presuppositions concerning truth. Interestingly, Richard Bauckham suggests that the most defining characteristic of the modern period was the pursuit of freedom in individual autonomy.[71] The modern world was primarily optimistic and as such it was convinced of the inevitability of progress. It put its faith in pedagogical progress. Learning, science, and technology would help solve most of the problems facing the world. Thomas Oden refers to this belief as "technological messianism."[72] The modern mind believed in the ability of man to deliver the utopia to which he aspired. This belief rested on a more fundamental presupposition that had faith in the inherent integrity of knowledge. It assumed a direct correlation between knowledge and improvement.

The modern era was also distinguished by Foundationalism. That is the view that "the world rests on a foundation of indubitable beliefs from which further propositions can be inferred to produce a superstructure of known truths."[73] Whether these foundations were self-evident truths or sense data, it was on the basis of such foundations that one could understand reality.[74] For Descartes, these primary and absolute principles were lucid and definite ideas: for David Hume they were sense experience. The modern period was one of epistemological certainty. D. A. Carson says, "the assumption for many thinkers in the period of modernity was that certainty, absolute epistemological certainty (and not just a psychological feeling), was not only desirable but attainable."[75]

Another essential feature of the modern period is its confidence in metanarratives to explain reality. Metanarratives are universal stories or accounts of reality that show how things really are.[76] Cahoone states that metanarratives are "philosophical stories, which legitimate all other discourse."[77] They demonstrate how knowledge and experience are interconnected and how they may be explicated. Jean-Francois Lyotard asserts that belief in metanarratives was the most essential feature of modernism.[78] World religions (obviously including Christianity) are seen as metanarratives as are philosophies and ideologies such as nationalism and Marxism. Hegel's theory of universal spirit is one example of a philosophical metanarrative.[79]

viii) The passing of modernism

McGrath notes, "Although a number of writers still maintain that modernism is alive and active, this attitude is becoming increasingly rare."[80] Most of these writers believe that modernism is in a serious tailspin and that the inexorable outcome will be its ultimate demise.[81] Anderson says that modernism has taken a serious fall, and he asserts that "Humpty-Dumpty is not going to be put back together again."[82] He argues that any attempt to do so is "ultimately self-defeating."[83] This does not mean that every aspect of modernism has ceased to exist, as Oden observes:

> It would be wrongheaded to infer that every aspect of modern consciousness is dead or that all social and political achievements of the last two centuries are lost. Modernity is not dead in the sense that all its repercussions and consequences are over, but in the sense that the ideological engine propelling the movement of modernity is broken down irreparably.[84]

Oden argues that many good aspects of modernism are still extant in literature, aesthetics, architecture, music, politics, civil liberties, medical advancements and new technologies.[85]

ix) Differences between modernism and postmodernism

The Enlightenment project brought new hope for many, seeing progress as inevitable and a bright future brought about through technological development. To Enlightenment thinkers, science became supreme and they believed that everything could be explained scientifically. In reaction to the premodern concepts of the gods and demons intervening and confusing lives, they argued that science provided answers to phenomena previously explained only by superstition.

It is important to clarify the essential differences between modernism and postmodernism because, as Carson points out, there is a tendency towards, "lumping all social change under one rubric."[86] In addition:

It is better, I think, to distinguish postmodernism from what might be called the *correlatives* of postmodernism. In other words it is more useful to define postmodernism fairly carefully, and then changes that fall outside that definition do not constitute postmodernism or serve as evidence of it or justify any particular thesis about postmodernism. The only alternative, as I have said, is so amorphous an approach that postmodern culture means nothing more than changing culture.[87]

Postmodernism is characterised by loss of confidence in the ability of reason to deliver the utopia that it seemed to promise. There is also a denial of the objectivity of knowledge. Knowledge is subjective and, therefore, relative and this involves a rejection of absolutes. Confidence in the inevitability of progress has been displaced with scepticism (if not cynicism). Foundationalism has been rejected and metanarratives have been cast aside as discredited worldviews. Language has come to be understood as a human construct. Tolerance is the spirit of the age and the acceptance of philosophical pluralism reflects this.

x) Loss of confidence in reason

The modernist mind believed in the power of reason. The modernist, therefore, had a faith in reason to deliver an objective understanding of knowledge and reality. That conviction and confidence which characterised modernism has been displaced with a disillusioned cynicism. McGrath says, "There has been a general collapse of confidence in the

Enlightenment trust in the power of reason to provide foundations for a
universally valid knowledge of the world, including God."[88] D. A. Carson
observes a certain "irony" in this trend. "The modernity which has
arrogantly insisted that human reason is the final arbiter of truth has
spawned a stepchild that has arisen to slay it."[89]

xi) Rejection of the objectivity of knowledge

Modernism's belief in the objectivity of knowledge has come to be
viewed as a discredited theory. Thus postmodernism denies the objectivity
of knowledge because it asserts that all knowledge is determined by
cultural and social factors. In the words of James B. Miller, "In the
postmodern context, all knowledge is viewed as cultural artefact."[90]

Postmodernism asserts that all knowledge is theoretical and the idea of
impartial, empirical facts is a modernist myth. Thus the cognitive capacity
of reason is an inadequate tool for objectively evaluating the world. Tarnas
notes, "Human knowledge is the historically contingent product of
linguistic and social practices of particular local communities of
interpreters, with no assured 'ever-closer' relation to an independent a-
historical reality."[91] Ronald J. Allen describes preaching as "interpretation"
and says, "We can never have access to statements that correspond in a
one-to-one fashion with reality. We only have access to interpretation of
the world."[92] Thus he suggests that, "the postmodern recognition of
perception as inherently interpretive suggests that conversation is an apt
way to think of preaching: the sermon is an event in which interpretation
takes place through conversation."[93] Recognising that, "The sermon is an
interpretation of the gospel in the context of the congregation"[94] should
stimulate the postmodern preacher to "find ways to listen to the
congregation and to bring their perceptions into the sermon."[95]

xii) Absolutely no absolutes

Richard Rorty says, "Tradition in Western culture...centres around the
notion of the search for Truth."[96] This "truth" is "something to be pursued
for its own sake."[97] One of the consequences of the loss of confidence in
reason and the denial of objective knowledge is a rejection of absolutes
especially the notion of absolute truth. The failure of reason to find
objective reality has led to a crisis in confidence which has given birth to a
cynical denial of absolute truth. Anderson notes, "Few of us realise that
even to hold a *concept* of relative truth makes us entirely different from
people who lived only a few decades ago."[98]

According to postmodernism the idea of absolute truth is an oppressive tool used by the powerful to exploit the weak.[99] The modernist perspective of absolute truth has led to the justification of the oppression and exploitation of others. Christopher Norris claims, "Postmodernism derives much of its suasive appeal from the notion that truth-claims are *always* on the side of some ultimate, transcendent, self-authorised Truth which excludes all meanings save those vouchsafed to the guardians of orthodox thought."[100] Belief in the universal and absolute nature of truth is seen as absurd in the postmodern perspective. The notion of universal truth and its exclusive claims is questioned and thought to be arrogant and intolerant. Anderson outlines the effect of this, "Once we let go of absolutes, nobody gets to have a position that is anything more than a position. Nobody gets to speak for God, nobody gets to speak for American values, and nobody gets to speak for nature."[101]

This has implications for Christianity. In addition to denying the concept of absolute truth, postmodernism asserts that "all religion reflects a historically conditioned bias."[102] Those with Christian convictions are less likely to face logical refutations of their beliefs than dismissal of them. Previously (in the modernist world) logic might be employed to refute the claims of Christianity. Postmodernists, however, do not contend in the same cognitive domain. Rather they dismiss Christianity's unique and universal claims as antiquated, arrogant and irrelevant. The notion of transcendent truth is despised, displaced or trivialised by relative truth. This has serious implications for the hermeneutics, exegesis and homiletics of both sacred and secular texts.

xiii) Loss of confidence in the inevitability of progress

Modernism placed its confidence in science and education to deliver a better world. Two world wars and numerous other conflagrations in which there have been acts of genocide have radically altered this view. Continuing famine, poverty, pollution and other calamities, together with racism and terrorism have demonstrated that progress is not the inexorable outcome of advances in science and education. The postmodernist, therefore, rejects what Oden calls "the smug fantasy of inevitable historical progress."[103]

Postmodernism acknowledges the modern era witnessed significant medical and technological breakthroughs but says that it has also brought "unparalleled potentiality for the demolition of humanity and the planet."[104] Again Henry points out, "The twentieth-century—the century of scientific progress—brought with it, among other debacles, World War

I, World War II, Marxist totalitarianism, Auschwitz, the increasing poisoning of the planet, and bare escape from nuclear destruction."[105] Nuclear, chemical and biological weapons of mass destruction threaten humanity. Thus postmodernists view many of modernism's technological advances as "a threat to planetary life and survival."[106]

Postmodernism not only rejects the idea of inevitable progress it also denies the modern faith in the inherent integrity of knowledge. It does not accept that there is a correlation between man's knowledge and munificence. Grenz notes "In the postmodern world, people are no longer convinced that knowledge is inherently good."[107] There has been a shift therefore, from the optimism that characterised the modern period to a pessimism that is the hallmark of postmodernism. For Oliver, this "can reflect cynicism in a world regarded as increasingly chaotic and out of control."[108]

xiv) Rejection of foundationalism

The view that there is a perpetual substructure to knowledge (foundationalism) has been critiqued and jettisoned by the postmodernist.[109] Henry observes that the rejection of foundationalism is the unique "epistemic premise" shared by all postmodernists.[110]

Foundationalism, which bases reality on universal truths and principles has been substituted by non-foundationalism. This is a "widespread attempt to continue philosophy without recourse to the kind of foundationalism found in classical modern philosophers."[111] Non-foundationalist philosophers in the school of Wittgenstein, Heidegger, and Rorty, dispute that philosophy can accomplish Cartesian certitude.[112] Thus philosophy may have pragmatic advantages but it cannot convey universal validity.

Adams notes that non-foundationalism seriously affects theology because it "seeks to disassociate theology from objective foundations such as Scripture, creeds and confessions, and ecclesiastical tradition."[113] With non-foundationalism, "theology arises out of the need of the community within the ever-changing contexts of culture and history."[114] If theology emerges from communal exigencies then Scripture, creeds, and church tradition cannot be a satisfactory foundation of theological activity.

xv) Deconstructionism

The optimism of the modern period was shattered by the nihilistic attacks of Friedrich Nietzsche (1844-1900) in the late nineteenth-century, though the final blows would not be felt until the 1970s.[115] Stanley Grenz wrote, "The immediate impulse for the dismantling of the Enlightenment project came from the rise of deconstruction as a literary theory, which influenced a new movement in philosophy."[116] Jacques Derrida is credited with being the "father of modern deconstruction". He is a philosopher who he has had a major impact in the field of literary criticism.[117]

Deconstruction, as a movement, arose in response to the "Structuralist" theory of interpreting literary texts. This theory suggested that cultures developed literature for the purpose of giving meaning to their existence, to make sense out of the meaninglessness of reality. The structuralists posited that all cultures utilise a common structure and by analysing this structure and reading the texts with this understanding makes sense out of experiences of reality.[118] "Post-structuralists" (who later adopted the title "Deconstructionists") rejected this view and argued that no such structure exists. All literature, according to this view, is dependent on the perspective of the reader. Meaning is derived from the text by entering into a dialogue with the text. Consequently there are as many readings of the text as there are readers. Deconstructionists have given postmodernists a tool for the advancement of their total rejection of the concept of objective truth.

Michel Foucault, another major proponent of deconstructionism, has taken deconstruction to another level by arguing that interpretations of truth are based on power. He suggests that at the root of every text or history there is someone who is advancing their position in order to oppress or subjugate those who are not in power.[119] Veith argues that, "Postmodern existentialism goes back to Neitzsche to emphasise not only will, but power. Liberation comes from rebelling against existing power structures, including oppressive notions of 'knowledge and 'truth'".[120] Foucault's position indicts every historian and writer with the charge of bias, and that bias is not only in order to further a cause, but ultimately to do violence to some oppressed group or culture. He claims that, "every assertion of knowledge is an act of power."[121] Foucault and other deconstructionists utilise a "hermeneutic of suspicion".[122] This means that as they interpret a text, they approach it with the suspicion that there may be a hidden agenda lurking somewhere in the background. Michel Foucault has argued that, "the concept of liberty is an invention of the ruling classes."[123] Taking his lead from Nietzsche, he suggests that the citizens think they are free, but are in fact being efficiently controlled by the ruling class. This is an example of how postmodernists employ the "hermeneutic of suspicion" in an examination of culture and truth to determine power structures that underlie various assumptions.

xvi) Rejection of metanarratives

Jean Francois Lyotard, one of the earliest defenders and commentators on postmodernism, defined the movement in terms of their total rejection of "metanarratives".[124] Harvey defines metanarratives as, "large scale theoretical interpretations purportedly of universal application."[125] They are "grand stories" that seek to explain reality in such a way that many individual ideas fit together in a comprehensive whole. In the modern period, these metanarratives represented a view that history is unfolding in certain kinds of patterns that shape understanding of the whole world. Christianity had its redemptive history in the death, burial and resurrection of Christ, as applicable to the whole world. Marx, borrowing from the Hegelian Dialectic, described all of history as a succession of economic revolutions.[126] The problem with metanarratives, argue postmodernists, is that they assume too much. They describe the world in such a way that all other parts of the world must subscribe to their way of thinking. Postmodernists reject the, "positivistic, technocentric, and rationalistic, universal modernism...identified with the belief in linear progress, absolute truths, the rational planning of social orders, and the standardization of knowledge and production."[127] They prefer instead, "heterogeneity and difference as liberative forces in the redefinition of cultural discourse."[128] Terry Eagleton summarises the attitude of postmodernists toward metanarratives:

> Post-modernism signals the death of such 'metanarratives' whose secretly terroristic function was to ground and legitimate the illusion of 'universal' human history. We are now in the process of wakening from the nightmare of modernity, with its manipulative reason and fetish of totality, into the laid back pluralism of the post-modern, that heterogeneous range of lifestyles and language games which has renounced the nostalgic urge to totalise and legitimate itself...Science and philosophy must jettison their grandiose metaphysical claims and view themselves more modestly as just another set of narratives.[129]

Although the issues discussed represent only a fraction of the ideas that could be considered under the title, "postmodern epistemology", these particular concepts are fairly representative of the key positions taken by postmodernists.

Metanarratives endeavour to support and clarify the nature of reality. Postmodernism rejects metanarratives as manipulative and exploitative. Jean-Francois Lyotard argues that postmodernism is best defined as "incredulity toward metanarratives."[130] Postmodernism rules out metanarratives because it discards all forms of "totalisation" and any form of striving toward rational coherence.[131] It does not permit a reality that is coherent and intelligible if it articulates an argument in a manner consistent with modernist absolute assumptions. So the use of metanarratives to explain reality is seen as both groundless and hazardous. Phillips and Ockholm state, "Postmodernism repudiates any appeal to Reality or Truth. The very attempt to propose totalizing metanarratives that define and legitimate Reality are denounced as oppressive."[132] Postmodernism does not permit metanarratives that claim to explicate reality because for it, absolute reality does not exist.

xvii) Language viewed as a human construct

Postmodernists argue that people are trapped in a world where no meaning is possible because humanity inhabits a "prison house of language".[133] This "prison" is a metaphor for the view that words have hidden trace meanings in them that communicate their opposite in order to oppress or exclude marginalised groups. For example, they point out that the word "man" is the opposite of "woman" and "freedom" is the opposite of "slavery". According to this view the use of the word "man" excludes and oppresses women. The words used contain the "trace" of the group being marginalised.[134] Postmodernists support their argument by noting that a free society would not need a word for freedom if there were no such thing as slavery.[135] Deconstructionism may have begun as a literary theory, but it has become a very sophisticated method of interpreting everything. Veith argues, "As it corrodes the very concept of absolute truth, deconstruction provides the intellectual grounding for the popular relativism running rampant in postmodern society."[136]

Utilising this tool of deconstruction, postmodernists have advanced new theories of truth. Jacques Derrida claims that meaning is not simply "out there" ready to be discovered. All that remains is the perspective of the interpreter.[137] Postmodernists renounce all claims to acquiring truth objectively. For them there is no absolute truth. They interpret truth relatively as "social constructs", and Foucault at least suggests the hidden motive of power behind all expressions of truth.

Philosopher Richard Rorty has abandoned the correspondence theory of truth. During the Enlightenment, truth was said to correspond with reality either by corresponding with innate ideas or sense data. The very idea that truth could be so easily determined is anathema to Rorty. He suggested abandoning the pursuit of "systematic philosophy" and replacing it with "edifying philosophy", which keeps up the dialogue, but ignores the search for truth.[138] Instead of a correspondence theory of truth, Rorty has defined truth as, "what our peers will let us get away with saying."[139] In other words, truth does not correspond or even cohere with reality. It only requires agreement from those equal in ability, standing and rank. Rorty, who considers himself a Pragmatist, has also adopted a pragmatic view of truth, suggesting that truth is, "what it is better for us to believe."[140] Once again he has abandoned modern conceptions of truth which require epistemic justification on more objective grounds.

Grenz writes that, "The postmodern worldview operates with a community-based understanding of truth."[141] He goes on to say that this worldview, "extends beyond our perceptions of truth to its essence: there is no absolute truth; rather truth is relative to the community in which we participate."[142] Stanley Fish says, "Communication does not take place in a vacuum, but in the context of the institutional community".[143] He argues that the meaning is not embedded in the text, but is derived in the context of the interpretive community.[144] In other words, even those who share the native language with the author cannot predict the precise meaning of a given text without having experienced the same context as the original author. For Fish and other postmodernists, the search for authorial intent is a futile exercise. Instead they advocate searching for meaning only within the interpretive community.

Kevin J. Vanhoozer argues that in the recent past there were "hard and fast lines between philosophy and literature."[145] This differentiation has become indistinct in the postmodern period, as language has come to be seen as a crucial constituent in how reality is understood. Horace L. Fairlamb notes, "Postmodernism is the time for which language is the game."[146]

In the postmodernist period, therefore, language is understood as a social construct whose significance is not inherent in reality. Seminal postmodern authors such as Jacques Derrida and Michel Foucault have reasoned that language is capricious and notional, and does not actually resonate any extraneous linguistic laws.[147] Language does not correspond to an objective other and texts are seen as constructs that neither describe nor define reality.[148] Language is a continuous system of artificial sign systems.[149]

There is a connection between postmodernism and deconstructionism.[150] Deconstruction is primarily about unpacking the constructions or explanations of language. Vanhoozer says, "It is about dismantling certain distinctions and oppositions that have traditionally guaranteed to philosophy its superior place among the humanities."[151] Essentially, therefore, deconstruction centres on the difficulty of linguistic representation.[152] As such, it is a challenge to what Derrida calls "logo-centrism." This is:

> ...the belief that there is some stable point *outside* language—reason, revelation, Platonic ideas—from which one can ensure that Deconstruction theory asserts that texts have no extra-linguistic basis or referent. As such the intended meanings of the author are deemed irrelevant to the interpretation of a text. If there are no legitimate interpretations of texts it follows one's words...correspond to the world.[153]

Logo-centrism, therefore, rests on the presupposition that one can speak truly.[154] That any interpretation may have equal validity or, on the other hand, they may be considered equally meaningless.[155] As mentioned earlier this has clear implications for secular and sacred textual analysis as the nature of hermeneutics and exegesis is fundamentally altered. Henry states:

> Texts are declared to be intrinsically incapable of conveying truth about some objective reality. One interpreter's meaning is as proper as another's, however incompatible these may be. There is no original or final textual meaning, no one way to interpret the Bible or any other text.[156]

The same could be said, for example, of the Koran. Language in postmodern theory is merely a functional tool.[157] There cannot be statements that are asserted to be true, in propositional terms, because it is not possible to prove or disprove them. It is merely a matter of linguistics. Cognitive comprehension, then, is merely a matter of individual perception and no understanding is absolute.[158]

xviii) Philosophical pluralism

Pluralism is a phenomenon that predates postmodernism. Various religions and cultures have always lived in close proximity. However, postmodernism has a particular relationship with contemporary pluralism. Henry observes, "Postmodernity approves pluralism as a necessary and desirable cultural and philosophical phenomenon."[159]

Philosophical pluralism contends that all religions have equal validity. No individual belief system is superior, and it is tolerant of most religions.[160] It abhors any religious system that makes exclusive claims concerning truth. Oliver says, "The postmodern attitude...rejects the idea that a rational belief system can claim authority over all others."[161] It is entirely intolerant of unique and universal religious truth claims. Thus the postmodern author, David Hall, states, "Dogmatism, totalitarianism, and narrow intolerance are all directly connected with unjustified claims to final truth."[162] Philosophical pluralism was not a feature of the modern period, as Anderson notes:

> A mere couple of centuries ago, most societies recognized a single official reality and dedicated themselves to destroying its opposition. You could get burned at the stake for suggesting that there might be more than one version of reality. Today, in some intellectual circles, you can get into trouble for suggesting there might be only one.[163]

xix) Postmodernism puts empirical science into question

Naturalism (the theory of the world that excludes the supernatural) as a system of belief has successfully made the transition from the modern era to the postmodern period.[164] It remains influential in spite of the fact that science no longer has the same "epistemological advantage."[165] Postmodernism, however, contests naturalism's presupposition that the universe is a self-contained unit.[166] It challenges the assumption of science that it can explain the existence of the universe by empirical means alone. Even the robust theories of David Hume and Immanuel Kant are subject to being critiqued. Allen observes, "Hume's and Kant's quite sophisticated objections that stood as intellectual orthodoxy for the past two hundred years have been found to fail."[167]

Thus William L. Rowe, writing from the position of the analytic school of philosophy, has contended that the notion of a self-contained universe can no longer be sustained by a philosophic consensus.[168] Recent debate about cosmology, especially the Big Bang theory, has raised questions concerning why this particular kind of universe has emerged. Allen says, "The question of why we have this universe rather than another has arisen *within* a branch of science itself for the first time in modern history."[169] This change within postmodernism is not exactly theism but it seems that the *embargo* on the potentiality of the existence of God has been lifted.[170]

Thus the concept of postmodernism is clarified by explaining areas of continuity and especially areas of discontinuity with its historical and philosophical precursors and progenitors. Postmodernism is essentially a philosophy that has responded pessimistically to the optimism of the Enlightenment and its principled certitude. The postmodern perspective of reality permeates contemporary culture and as such "postmodern" is an appropriate appellation for contemporary culture. Its loss of confidence in reason and its rejection of the objectivity of knowledge distinguish postmodernism from modernism. There are no absolutes, and there is widespread cynicism regarding belief in inexorable progress. This spirit of disillusionment is evident in the denial of the inherent goodness of knowledge. Foundationalism is forsaken and metanarratives are dismissed as myths that serve the purposes of the powerful in manipulating and exploiting the disadvantaged. Christianity is deemed to be a metanarrative and is cast off as an inadequate explanation of reality. The idea that language has extra-linguistic referents is no longer accepted and philosophical pluralism is espoused. The view that the universe is self-contained has been challenged as an unwarranted assumption.

The title of Anderson's book, *Reality Isn't What it Used to Be,* encapsulates something of the uncertainty that characterises the postmodern era. It may be a feature of the world for a long time to come, or it may introduce something else to take its place. One wonders what will follow postmodernism. Certainly, its philosophical presuppositions have dramatically changed the way in which many people view the world.

Stanley Grenz says that postmodernism, "signifies the quest to move beyond modernism. Specifically, it involves a rejection of the modern mind-set, but launched under the conditions of modernity."[171] This suggests that postmodernism is a reaction to modernity and that it involves a cultural shift that has its origins within modernity. The modern mind-set was born in the age of the Enlightenment when "the triumph of reason and the mastery of the human mind over the external world" were thought to have delivered modern man from the dark ages.[172] David Harvey points out that:

> Enlightenment thought embraced the idea of progress, and actively sought that break with history and tradition which modernity espouses. It was, above all, a secular movement that sought the demystification and desacralization of knowledge and social organisation in order to liberate human beings from their chains.[173]

As this comment suggests, the pre-modern period was often characterised by mystical and sacred explanations for reality. The Enlightenment project sought to shift culture from what was considered archaic and inaccurate understandings of reality in the "pre-modern" period to a modern age of Enlightenment. In a similar shift, postmodernism is an attempt to move beyond modernism.

To pick up on a thread from earlier in the discussion it should be borne in mind that there is disagreement among scholars as to whether the term "postmodernism" is an accurate term for the phenomena witnessed in contemporary culture.[174] The term has met with varying degrees of support and rejection even among those who first began to write about the phenomena. Lyon points out that since the 1980s, and "despite the fact several of these discarded, denied or distanced themselves" from it, the term "postmodern" came to be linked to their name.[175] However, in spite of the fact that postmodernists have accepted the term and many authors have used the term in their descriptions of current cultural phenomena, there are a number of prominent thinkers and writers who are unwilling to accept "postmodernism" as a descriptive term for the cultural shift. Harold Netland, among others, uses the terminology of "postmodernism" for the sake of argument but he is unwilling to adopt its use for the conditions now prevalent in our culture. He points out that:

> Since the 1970's, the term postmodern has been used in a variety of literary, philosophical, social and political trends linked by their critique of established 'modern' values, assumptions and institutions. Postmodernity in this sense refers to a broad range of late-twentieth-century intellectual and cultural movements in the fine arts, architecture, communications media, politics, the social sciences, literary theory and hermeneutics, and philosophy that perhaps are more connected by what they reject than by what they affirm.[176]

He argues that this paradigm which understands postmodernity as a repudiation of modernity and the Enlightenment project is reductionistic.[177] He wrote that, "identifying modernity with the Enlightenment tends to minimise other intellectual movements of the time, thereby granting it more influence than it deserves."[178] He sees the Enlightenment project as unfinished and continuing and suggests that this ongoing process of modernisation and globalisation should be called, "the culture of modernity".

The changes in culture that have come about as a result of modernisation and globalisation are profound. Technological improvements have facilitated travel and thereby created a global village. The boundaries between local, national and international communities have become blurred. The changes that have resulted from worldwide communication through television and the internet have also brought together diverse cultures from every corner of the globe. It should be noted that globalisation is not just a Western phenomenon. The cultures of the Eastern world are interacting with the cultures of the Western world, so that both are experiencing the influences of each other moving in both directions simultaneously.[179] Netland is not alone in contending that the word postmodernity inaccurately portrays the phenomena being witnessed today.

Thomas Oden takes a similar view and argues that the culture shift being currently experienced should be categorised as "ultramodernity" rather than postmodernity.[180] The impact of modernisation and globalisation have pushed the boundaries of modernity but the current cultural shift is moving away from some key ideals of modernity while employing the forces of modern cultural change to bring about a new cultural and social paradigm. It is reductionistic to suggest that postmodernity is now the prevailing view of contemporary culture. It is not a complete repudiation of modernity. The shift toward postmodernity is more gradual. Global culture is experiencing a shift that repudiates some aspects of modernity, while retaining and even extending other aspects of modernity to new levels. In spite of these areas of disagreement the term "postmodernism" will be used to describe the current philosophical and cultural shift. Since many of the proponents of this cultural shift have adopted the use of the term and as the data demonstrates a degree of repudiation of modernity there is warrant for using the term to describe the phenomena.

It is necessary, however, to identify the kind of modernism that postmodernists are reacting to when they suggest moving beyond modernism. David Harvey has pointed out that the epistemological assumptions of the Enlightenment project are at the heart of a kind of modernism that postmodernists reject. He has written:

> The Enlightenment, for example, took as its axiomatic that there was only one possible answer to any question. From this it followed that the world could be controlled and rationally ordered if we could only picture and represent it rightly. But this presumed that there existed a single correct mode of representation which, if we could uncover it (and this was what scientific and mathematical endeavours were all about), would provide the means to Enlightenment ends.[181]

Grenz concurs with this analysis and points out that foundational to the Enlightenment project was the assumption that "knowledge is certain, objective and good."[182] These particular assumptions of the Enlightenment have been repudiated by postmodernists. Enlightenment thinkers argued that certainty in knowledge can be achieved through human reason alone and objectivity can be achieved by observing the world as "unconditioned observers."[183] In addition, Enlightenment thinkers developed the idea that knowledge is inherently good. In this they were optimistic in their assumptions. Grenz has noted that this led them to the belief that, "progress is inevitable, that science, coupled with the power of education will free us from our vulnerability to nature, as well as from all social bondage."[184] Postmodernists reject these epistemological assumptions of the Enlightenment, but as already noted they have retained certain aspects of modernity so that both postmodernity and modernity have a continuing influence on contemporary culture. Epistemological issues provide a framework for understanding postmodern thought and will influence the development of an approach to preaching.

xx) Alternative logic

In addition to alternative views of truth, postmodernists have advanced an alternative view of logic. During the Enlightenment it would have been unthinkable to assert that two opposing views could both be true. Aristotle developed the systematic principles of logic that most of the western world has subscribed to for centuries. In deductive logic, Aristotle developed three principles: the law of identity, the law of non-contradiction and the law of the excluded middle. The law of identity states simply that: A stands for A. The law of non-contradiction states that something cannot be both A and not-A at the same time. The law of excluded middle says that something is either A or not-A. Derrida and others have challenged this view of logic.[185] They are more than willing to accept contradiction, and indeed seem to celebrate contradictory logic as if it frees them from the constraints of modernity.

Why do they take this position? It seems in part to reflect their total system of thought. They believe that truth is culturally and socially constructed. As the argument goes, since there are no absolute truths, people can hold to different "truths". Veith points out that, "Existentialism provides the rationale for contemporary relativism. Since everyone creates his or her own meaning, every meaning is equally valid", no matter how contradictory they may be.[186] The common refrain is, "what's true for you may not be true for me."[187]

xxi) A critique of postmodern epistemology

There are some positive elements in postmodernism that may provide a basis for dialogue with those who espouse religious views. It is important that any critique of postmodernism should also identify the common ground between what appears to be two diametrically opposed positions.

Postmodernists may be commended for their sympathetic attitude toward the oppressed and marginalised. It may be affirmed that truth has sometimes been used to oppress. There are elements of deconstruction which have proved helpful in discerning ways that history has been written to uphold the powerful and suppress the weak. Believers can affirm them in that quest for more accurate historical analysis.

Michel Foucault's emphasis on the use of "power" to establish truth has some warrant and can also be affirmed. Those who are in power are often guilty of manipulating the truth to suit their own ends.[188] Postmoderns can be affirmed in their practice of employing a "hermeneutic of suspicion" when reading a text. Knowledge is conditioned by point of view. Everybody has paradigms and ways of viewing reality that are often shaped by upbringing and culture, just as experiences in life affect judgements and attitudes. Presuppositions must be taken into consideration, and positions held must be carefully evaluated with the understanding that what is held to be true may in fact be "tinted" by the colour of the lenses used to view reality.

Postmodernists can also be fêted for their celebration of diversity and disdain for prejudice. People of faith should logically be the greatest champions of this enterprise. Postmodernists, along with others, have levelled complaints against religion for the oppression of marginalised groups and those complaints are not without warrant. For example, Christian missionary enterprises have been somewhat culpable in various colonial injustices. Colonising nations have stripped the raw materials of their colonies and enslaved the indigenous peoples, attempting at the same time to evangelise them. The criticism, that Christianity looks more like an oppressive power than a religion of freedom and love, has merit. Christians have been ethnocentric and prejudiced and indeed Christian nations continue to exploit and abuse other nations in this postcolonial world where the corporate benefactors of politicians set the agenda for economics without ethics.

Christians can affirm, with postmodernists, that they are guilty of arbitrarily ascribing right and wrong to certain acts, based solely on self interest rather than truly discerning an absolute right or absolute wrong based on objective criteria.

Christians cannot claim to have a monopoly on the debate on truth, and the nature of right and wrong. There is a great deal of hypocrisy in the manner in which Christianity is practiced, and believers have much to learn about morality. There has been a great deal of emphasis in the Western Christian church on private (especially sexual) morality, but less attention has been given to issues of social injustice and structural inequalities. The very people who are most likely to protest about moral relativism are often guilty of practicing moral relativism when it suits their own self-interests.

Not every claim of postmodernism, therefore, is without warrant. There is much that Christians can learn from postmodernism. Many postmodern attacks against modernity are points of agreement with faith, and are a welcome relief after generations of embattling apologetics. For example, believers and postmodernists agree that science does not have all the answers. Human beings are not just material objects, smart animals which are evolutionarily more highly developed, but basically part of a mechanistic universe. The main world religions affirm a grander metanarrative than this, that understands God as the Creator and sustainer of the universe.

Christianity and postmodernism agree that "progress" has its negative side: science's development of nuclear weapons, for example. Christianity and postmodernism are agreed that there are some things that cannot be known, based on perception alone. Believers would place knowing God in this category. Postmodernists may not necessarily affirm the existence of God but the allowance for non perceptual beliefs leaves room for this assertion. Christians (and indeed other religious adherents; for example, those of the other two Abrahamic world religions: Judaism, and Islam) and postmodernists can agree that reason alone is insufficient for discerning the veracity of truth claims. While postmodernists reject the idea that there is an objective truth, and Christians affirm revelation, both find reason alone insufficient, and in this there can be agreement.[189]

On the other hand, there are, undeniably, serious areas of disagreement, such as the rejection of objective truth. The basis for the rejection of objective truth takes as its starting point the rejection of classical foundationalism. It should be noted that the rejection of classical foundationalism, and attempts to find a more accurate form of epistemic justification, is one of the most important issues in contemporary philosophy.[190] Postmodernists are not alone in their rejection of classical foundationalism; many contemporary philosophers have also rejected it. However, they have not taken the next step and rejected all objective truth. The postmodern rejection of classical foundationalism is justified because classical foundationalism is inherently flawed.[191] However, for a postmodernist to reject all forms of epistemic justification is unwarranted. Alvin Plantinga has written:

> Postmodernists nearly all reject classical foundationalism; in this they concur with most Christian thinkers and most contemporary philosophers. Momentously enough, however, many postmodernists apparently believe that the demise of classical foundationalism implies something far more startling: that there is no such thing as truth at all.[192]

Some of the tenets of postmodernism may be affirmed, as noted earlier, such as the practice of deconstruction, especially regarding the use of power to oppress those at the margins of society. As already observed the fact that those in power sometimes oppress the marginalised should arouse caution or even suspicion. But postmodern deconstruction goes too far. If every text, history and statement must be deconstructed, then deconstruction itself may also be deconstructed. As such postmodern deconstruction is subject to its own ideological and methodological rules.[193]

Derrida has reserved "justice" as the one area that is exempt from deconstruction. He argues that, "Justice is not deconstructible. After all not everything is deconstructible, or there would be no point to deconstruction."[194] It appears arbitrary to exempt justice, and it makes deconstruction self-referentially defeated on two counts. Firstly, deconstruction as a methodology could not survive its own deconstruction. Secondly, the exemption suggested by Derrida seems to be another example of the use of power to assert truth. Derrida's tool is supposed to cut away power biases but he reserves the power to exempt certain components (justice and deconstruction itself) from the process. This is a fatal flaw.

Postmodernists also reject a correspondence theory of truth, and representationalism (an important corollary of epistemic justification). It has been stated that correspondence theory is the belief that truth corresponds with reality. It may now be added that representationalism is the view that truth represents reality. If what is believed about reality has no foundations or cannot be epistemically justified, then truth is called into question as well. Rorty's definition of truth is intrinsically flawed.[195] Since he has rejected objectivity and a correspondence view of truth, he has left himself an easy prey for his peers, such as Louis Pojman who stated, "I won't let him get away with saying that."[196] Rorty, by his own definition of truth, has painted himself into a corner, so that his definition of truth is itself false. If for him his definition of truth is, "what our peers will let us get away with saying" and his peers won't let him get away with that definition, then his view of truth fails.

Rorty's other definition of truth also has significant problems. He has said that truth is, "what is better for us to believe."[197] This shows his pragmatism. When taken to its ultimate logical conclusion this view of truth leads to radical pluralism and relativism. If truth is what is better for one to believe then there is nothing inhibiting one from creating truth to suit ones self-interest. Alvin Plantinga has made a similar argument against this view of truth. He offers three analogies of how this view of truth distorts reality and ultimately leads to erroneous ways of thinking. In the analogy of A.I.D.S., for instance, a person may decide to believe there was no such thing as this disease. His colleagues may let him get away with saying that and it may seem better to him to believe this way. According to Rorty, then, A.I.D.S. no longer exists. Plantinga's second example points out that in the Tiananmen Square debacle, the Chinese authorities denied that students were murdered. According to Rorty's view, if other authorities would let them get away with saying it never occurred, then the truth would be that it never happened. With regard to the Holocaust, there are neo-Nazi groups who deny it occurred. According to Rorty's view of truth if their peers allow them to get away with saying this then it becomes true.[198]

This postmodern view of truth is cast as something socially constructed.[199] The idea is that truth is created within a community or social group, and that community's truth is true for them. While an outsider may criticise their version of truth, these criticisms are invalid, since it is true for them. This radical reshaping of truth, apart from correspondence or coherence theory, has sweeping implications for society and especially the Christian church and other major religions. To radically redefine truth as it suits the individual or the social group does violence to every institution and every member of society. Postmodernists will argue that two cultures cannot effectively communicate with each other because their languages are different.[200] Postmodernists confuse the relativity of the term selection, "with an inability of language to represent objective reality."[201] This is a huge leap. On this view of socially constructed truth, the argument follows that belief in God is a social construct and therefore God's existence is dependent on the existence of the society that believes in God. In other words if nobody believed in God, then God would not exist. Plantinga argues, "This claim on Rorty's part will constitute a defeater...only if he also makes us aware of some reason why we should believe it."[202] Rorty's claims cannot survive their own internal inconsistencies and are self-referentially defeating.

Rorty suggests that truth can be created by making propositional statements. Plantinga critiques this idea. Believers assert that God created the world. Rorty's view is that statements bring truth into being. Thus believers are responsible not only for making the statement that God created the world, but also for creating the world.[203]

It has been already noted that there is also a problem in postmodernism with respect to logic but this needs further comment. The postmodernist attempt to deconstruct all of modernity has involved rejecting the laws of logic, including the law of non-contradiction, which states that something cannot be true and at the same time false. Rorty's views of truth allows for such contradictions between individuals and communities. He is saying more than, there are different versions of the truth based on diverse perspectives.[204] It is one thing to say that a pre-modern culture may be epistemologically justified in believing what their ancestors have taught them; it is quite another to say that their version of the truth is true, when it stands in contradiction to the objectively verifiable reality of modern culture. This is not to say that just because of the Enlightenment, all modern truth is to be taken as a settled issue. But modernity has given insight that cannot be rejected outright. Derrida would argue that this statement is another example of the bias of power, the arrogance of modernity. It is not that modernity has all the answers, but that both cultures cannot both be right about the same issue. That violates the law of non-contradiction: A cannot be A, and at the same time, not A.

This postmodern rejection of logic has implications that go beyond evaluating cultures. In the arena of morality, postmodern alternative "logic" suggests that each individual culture and for that matter each individual may choose what is right and wrong for themselves, even when those moral choices stand in direct contradiction to other standards of behaviour. Rorty's view that "what works better for me" means, in theory, that an individual may say, "stealing works better for me than working" and that is an acceptable morality for postmodernists. Postmodernists are not typically religious. However, their views of truth and reality allow for two contradictory religions to make truth claims that are exclusive and accept both as right and true. Thus postmodernism is internally and essentially inconsistent, self-referentially incoherent and contradictory. It neither has the coherence to convince nor the cogency to compel universal allegiance.

One final tenet of postmodernism deserves to be critiqued; that is the rejection of metanarratives. Postmodernists reject any all-encompassing story that seeks to paint the whole picture of reality. Instead they posit mini-narratives or "petit-narratives".[205] These are the stories of individual cultures that explain reality for them, without suggesting that they encompass other cultures or the whole world. Christianity is a metanarrative because it explains reality in relation to the origin, purpose and destiny of mankind and spans many cultures and all classes.

Postmodernists pour scorn on religious metanarratives. However, if their scorn is primarily focused on forms of oppression of the marginalised and the promotion of the self-interests of a privileged few, then religion must work harder to demonstrate that the religious metanarratives are different. This will involve much more than improvements in personal piety; it will involve dismantling the structures of globalisation, challenging institutional inequities, radically working toward the transforming of international relations (especially in the area of world trade) and the realisation that empowering others will involve a coterminous disempowering of privileged elites, be they individuals, communities or nations. People who say that Western Christianity does not oppress the marginalised are either naïve or in denial about structural poverty. Much of the prosperity of Western nations is based on the exploitation of peoples in the third world. Much of this oppression is done by "Christian" nations.

The Christian metanarrative is not intended to maintain the power of privileged elites. Christianity's unbalanced emphasis on personal piety and its failure to emphasise social justice is part of the problem. The church has spawned a child that is angry with the rhetoric of love and the reality of neglect. Certain expressions of religion have been oppressive and abusive and postmodernists have some warrant in holding them in contempt. However, postmodernists have built their own metanarrative. Their view of truth, reality, history and morality is effectively a metanarrative. The postmodernist is guilty of the same charge levelled at the Christian metanarrative insofar as it is a system of thought used to determine reality. Postmodernists insist that their view has universal validity and application and in so doing they are effectively defining it as a worldview which is a metanarrative. At best they can say it is not an "oppressive" metanarrative, except that those who believe in the existence of absolute universal truth might feel oppressed by such a claim. The postmodernist would contend that their view allows for different cultures to make individual truth claims, but postmodernism is nevertheless a methodological tool for interpreting reality, and as such, subject to its own criticisms.

In this chapter postmodernism has been explored from a historical and philosophical perspective with a view to providing a critique of the epistemological views held by postmodernists. It has been stated that postmodernism represents a challenge to the church in general and to preaching in particular but it does not present an insurmountable challenge to belief. It has been suggested that the seeds of that system's ultimate demise have been planted in its epistemology. It has been established that postmodernism rejects objective truth claims, but it does so, and indeed must do so, by *making* objective truth claims. It deconstructs truth and reality, but insists that deconstruction is exempt from deconstruction. Postmodernism argues for an alternative system of logic, but by its own definition of logic, this alternative view of logic would be both true and false. Postmodernism rejects metanarratives, but it must do so by building a new metanarrative. In the final analysis, postmodern philosophy appears to be self-referentially incoherent. Nevertheless, it remains as a prevalent worldview, and presents both new challenges and new opportunities for people of faith and in particular, preaching practitioners.

xxii) The popularisation of postmodernism

Reality and truth have been called into question, not just by postmodern philosophers, but by ordinary people. The advances in science with the theory of relativity, super-string theory and the discovery of quantum mechanics and quarks, has caused this new generation to wonder if they really know anything for sure. Postmodern thought is becoming more widespread, and affecting society as a whole, and not just in an academic context.[206] Graham Johnston notes, "Postmodern thinking creeps into our lives not necessarily through conscious choices but through a steady stream of bombardment via movies, magazines, song and television."[207] Moral relativism is both a feature of modernity and postmodernity. However it could be argued that moral relativism in postmodernity developed a new dimension as a result of the epistemological issues that have emerged in postmodernity. For example, in modernity the move to supplant revelation with reason suggested that morality could be based on rational grounds such as Kant's categorical imperative. In postmodernity, morality has no basis in either revelation or reason, but has become socially constructed so that the community is entitled to affirm their own version of morality without reference to any authority other than the group with which they associate.

Popular television demonstrates the prevalence of postmodernism even in the more cerebral shows. Stanley Grenz has written a piece entitled, "Star Trek and the Next Generation: Postmodernism and the Future", in which he points out the shift in worldview between the older *Star Trek* series and *Star Trek: The Next Generation*. In the Older show a key character was Spock, who was an alien (half Vulcan and half human). His personal struggle between the Vulcan logical self and his human emotional self is the centrepiece of the character and created some evocative drama. He represented a human without emotions, totally scientific and rational, a paragon of modernity. In *The Next Generation*, the equivalent character is Data, an android that longs to become human, but has capabilities that far surpasses all human beings.[208] His search for humanity and his repudiation of emotionless rationality, Grenz argues, points to the postmodern shift in society. Further comparisons can be made. In the older series time was linear; in the newer series time is fluid and many of the most interesting shows involve some form of non-linear, space-time fluctuations that produce all sorts of interesting paradoxes. There is also a postmodern flavour to the "Prime Directive" which states that they are not to interfere with other cultures. This brings to mind the ideas of Foucault and Derrida, for whom every encounter with another culture has the prospect of imposing truth upon others based on a bias of power.

The emergence of postmodernism can also be seen in the legal arena. In the USA, during the Clarence Thomas hearings conducted to determine whether or not to confirm his nomination to the Supreme Court, Thomas' religious background was examined. His background in Roman Catholic parochial schools was explored and some of the more liberal justices wondered if his view of right and wrong might be grounded in natural theology, the idea that morality is inherent in the universe. After much debate the chairman of the committee instructed Thomas, "Right and wrong are what the United States Congress decides."[209] It appears that the Western system of jurisprudence established on the Judeo-Christian ethic is beginning to change its values.

How did postmodernism enter the mainstream? It has already been noted that the mass media has contributed toward a wider acceptance of postmodern views. However, many scholars have attempted to determine how these philosophical views began to emerge in mainstream culture. David Harvey represents the prevailing view that the counter-cultural movements of the 1960's with their anti-modernistic perspectives give rise to postmodernism in contemporary culture. He writes:

> Antagonistic to the oppressive qualities of scientifically grounded technical-bureaucratic rationality…the counter-cultures explored the realms of individualized self-realization through a distinctive 'new left' politics, through the embrace of anti-authoritarian gestures, iconoclastic habits (in music, dress, language and lifestyle), and the critique of everyday life.[210]

Harvey goes on to suggest that this particular counter-cultural movement which began in universities, art institutes and on the cultural fringes of large cities, eventually spilled out into all the major cities and became a mainstream movement in Western culture.[211] Veith also attributes the rise of postmodernism with the counter-cultural movement of the 1960's and adds that, "the young people began questioning the fruits of modern civilization…They sought instead a way of life organically related to nature and free of moral and rational constraints."[212] He adds that during that period young people experimented with drugs and, "cast off sexual prohibitions to realize total freedom and to pursue a life of untrammelled pleasure."[213] If their assessment is accurate, then the epistemological views of postmodernists became the paradigm that allowed the counter-cultural movement of the 1960's to find the liberation from the constraints of modernity that they had been seeking.

xxiii) Areas of further investigation

As mentioned in the title, this chapter is a *preliminary* discussion of issues pertaining to the feasibility of the homiletic task in postmodern culture. Understanding postmodernism is a necessary prerequisite to formulating an apologetic strategy for effectively communicating with the contemporary mind.[214] This chapter has focused primarily on an initial discussion of the issues. It is, therefore, a preliminary inquiry insofar as it provides a foundation for further investigation of ideas of truth and revelation in the light of postmodernism. This is a first step toward understanding the contemporary challenge (its problems and possibilities) and selecting an approach to preaching that is cognisant of the new epistemology. This calls for an assessment of theological theories and preaching models beginning with a comparative analysis of narrative, topical and expository preaching and also an examination of inductive and deductive modes of preaching Christ in a postmodern culture.[215]

CHAPTER THREE

DEVELOPING AN APPROACH TO PREACHING WHICH IS COGNIZANT OF POSTMODERN CULTURE

There are some, and perhaps many, situations where preaching is powerful and effective. It cannot, however, be said that this is what is happening in every local church. Capill makes the following observation:

> In many a church you can find preaching that is topical and contemporary, but light on biblical substance. You can easily find preaching that is personal, but in a largely subjective or emotional way. You may well find preaching that is solidly biblical, yet rather lifeless and dreary. But to find clear, powerful preaching of the Word that grips your heart and leaves you not so much feeling that you have been in the presence of a great communicator as in the presence of a great God, not so much entertained by a man as enthralled by the truth of God—that, it seems is all to rare. [1]

There is a multiplicity of reasons for this particular state of affairs.

i) The role of knowledge in the Christian faith

Throughout its history the church has confessed that God has, "revealed himself, not only in creation and providence, not only in Jesus Christ, but also verbally and informationally."[2] This foundational belief has been questioned and in many instances discarded, thus having an effect on the role of preaching. Many present-day theologians are questioning man's ability to attain knowledge about God.[3] This agnostic attitude toward God can be seen in the writings of Gordon Kaufman:

> The real reference for 'God' is never accessible to us or in any way open to our observation or experience. It must remain always an unknown X, a mere limiting idea with no content. It stands for the fact that God transcends our knowledge in modes and ways of which we can never be aware and of which we have no inkling...God is ultimately profound

Mystery and utterly escapes our every effort to grasp or comprehend him.
Our concepts are at best metaphors and symbols of his being, not literally
applicable.[4]

This kind of scepticism is also apparent in the writings of philosopher
W. T. Stace who maintained that: "God is utterly and forever beyond the
reach of logical intellect or of any intellectual comprehension, and that in
consequence when we try to comprehend his nature intellectually,
contradictions appear in our thinking."[5] These views have trivialised the
traditional role that truth has played in Christian religion. Cognitive
reflection about God is declared impossible, and replaced by personal
encounter, religious feeling, trust or obedience.[6] In other words, "God does
not give us information by communication. He gives us Himself in
communion. It is not information about God that is revealed but...God
Himself".[7] William Temple held that, "there is no such thing as revealed
truth…What is offered to man's apprehension in any specific revelation is
not truth concerning God but the living God Himself."[8] This marked a
dramatic break from traditional historic Christianity, a tradition that
affirmed both an intelligible revelation from God and the divinely given
human ability to know the transcendent God through the medium of true
propositions.

Ronald Nash says that the possibility of human knowledge about God
has been denied on at least three grounds: (1) some have precluded
knowledge about God on the basis of particular theories about the nature
of human knowledge; (2) others have been led to antagonism because of
their view of the nature of God.[9] An example of this is that some have so
exaggerated the divine transcendence that the Wholly Other God of whom
they speak could not be an object of human knowledge; and (3) still others
have affirmed the impossibility of knowledge about God because of
theories about the nature of human language, whereby language is
regarded as incapable of serving as an adequate conveyor of information
about God.

He asks whether there is a relationship between the human mind and
the divine mind that is sufficient to ground the communication of truth
from God to humans. He further states that there was no doubt in Christian
thought that such a relationship exists, and that such a relationship is
possible until "alien" theories of knowledge gained ascendancy in the
decades after Hume and Kant.[10] If there is no communication of truth
possible from God to humans, then this has serious implications for the
preacher who intends to use the Bible as an authoritative source of
knowledge about God, and a means of inspiring greater vitality of faith in
God and a deeper and richer encounter of God.

ii) An emphasis on feelings

Kant's rejection of the possibility of cognitive knowledge of God was taken up by various thinkers, such as, Friedrich Schleiermacher (1768-1834) and Albrecht Ritschl (1822-1889), both of whom became major sources of Protestant liberalism. Schleiermacher thought of his own work as a reaction against Kant's reduction of religion to an ethical exercise of the will. But despite his protests against Kant, Schleiermacher's position in the end became an extension of Kant's theological agnosticism.[11]

Schleiermacher distinguished between the kernel and the husk of religion suggesting that many of the cultured despisers of religion in his day were in fact offended by the nonessential elements of Christianity. The dispensable husk of religion, in his view, included the metaphysical theories and theological doctrines so many unbelieving intellectuals found incredible. Schleiermacher wrote:

> For what are these doctrinal structures, these systems of theology, these theories about the origin and the end of the world, these analyses concerning the nature of an incomprehensible being? Here everything elapses into callous argumentation. Here the sublimest subjects are made pawns of controversy between competing schools of thought. Now surely…this is not the character of religion.[12]

Schleiermacher went on to reject two approaches to religion. Firstly, he attacked those who thought of religion primarily as a way of thinking or knowing something. Secondly, he rejected those who, like Kant, viewed religion primarily as a way of living or doing; as a kind of conduct or character. For Schleiermacher, religion must not be confused either with knowing or with doing. He believed that true religion is found in feeling.[13] He wrote:

> Faith must be something quite different from a mishmash of opinions about God and the world (the theoretical approach) or a collection of commands for one life or two (the practical way of Kant). Piety must be something more than the craving after this hodgepodge of metaphysical and moral crumbs…[14]

Schleiermacher went on to reinterpret Christian theology in terms of his emphasis on religious feeling. He did this in a two-volume work, *The Christian Faith*, where he expanded his conviction that the essence of religion is to be found in a human being's feeling of absolute dependence.[15]

Schleiermacher came to be regarded as the fountainhead of one dominant form of liberalism, namely, the view that it does not matter what a person believes, it is what he feels that is important. It is clear that he thought it wrong to regard revelation as any kind of human discovery. Revelation is not something, "excogitated in thought by one man and so learned by others."[16] Wells points out that Schleiermacher, "repudiated objective knowledge of God and then, like the Romantics, reached down into his own being to find the grounding for his knowledge of God."[17] It seems that this kind of subjective theological emphasis has effectively "cultivated the soil" to receive the "seeds" of postmodernism.

iii) The emerging church

During the last two decades a new movement has been sweeping across America and the United Kingdom and spreading internationally; this relatively new phenomenon is identified as the "emerging" or "emergent" church.[18] At the heart of the "movement", or as some people prefer to call it, the "conversation" says Carson:

> ...lies the conviction that changes in culture signal that a new church is 'emerging'. Christian leaders must, therefore adapt to this emerging church. Those who fail to do so are blind to the cultural accretions that hide the gospel behind forms of thought and modes of expression that no longer communicate with the new generation.[19]

Gerald K. Weber gives some insight into understanding this emerging church:

> On the crest of a postmodernism wave rides a new movement called the emerging (or emergent) church. It's essentially a Generation-X happening ... despite the volume of material in books and blogs, little about the emerging church is organised. Some adherents call it a conversation. Still this trend cannot be ignored. Every week followers gather to drink coffee, listen to Christian music, and hear a story-sermon under church names like The Journey, Pierced Chapel and The Scum of the Earth Church.[20]

As the emerging church is essentially a postmodern phenomenon, Weber's observations are particularly relevant. He says that the emerging church, "defies definition...is driven by disappointment...deprecates doctrine...is deficient in discernment...dotes on devotion and is destined for disuse."[21] Even proponents of the emerging church have difficulty defining it. Leonard Sweet says, "Our faith is ancient. Our faith is future. We're old fashioned. We're new fangled. We're orthodox. We're innovators. We're postmodern Christians."[22] Elsewhere Sweet observes that Christian spirituality is, "anything but sane if sane means, logical, predictable, serious or safe. Christian spirituality is highly illogical, paradoxical, volatile, playful and dangerous..."[23]

At the heart of the emerging church is a protest movement which is disillusioned with the previous three or four generations. They have respect for ancient forms and traditions but feel that their modern forebears have failed them. Carson agrees, describing the common thread of protest as, "we were where you were once, but we emerged from it into something different."[24] Emergents are typical postmoderns inasmuch as they dislike absolutism and reject what they call "rational" preaching, dogmatic teaching, confrontational evangelism and adversarial apologetics. They prefer relationships to programmes and are determined to replace the latter with the former and refer to this as the, "rebooting of the church".

The fact that emergents despise doctrine reflects a postmodern mindset and as such they prefer a "whatever-works-for-you" approach to theology. One website states, "The modern creedal orientation of 'we believe' has been subverted by the postmodern creedal orientation summed up by Sheryl Crow in her song which proclaims, 'If it makes you happy it can't be half bad.'"[25] Albert Mohler observes:

> The Emergent movement represents a significant challenge to biblical Christianity. Unwilling to affirm that the Bible contains propositional truths that form the framework for Christian belief, this movement argues that we can have Christian symbolism and substance without those thorny questions of truthfulness that have so vexed the modern mind. The worldview of postmodernism – complete with an epistemology that denies the possibility of or need for propositional truth—affords the movement an opportunity to hop, skip and jump throughout the Bible and the history of Christian thought in order to take whatever pieces they want from one theology and attach them, like doctrinal post-it notes, to whatever picture they would want to draw.[26]

Concerning the criticism that the emerging church is not very discerning; it should be noted that this movement has attracted many intelligent and articulate adherents.[27] One of its most eloquent spokespersons is writer and Masters graduate Brian McLaren, pastor of Cedar Ridge Community Church in Spencerville, Maryland in the U.S.A. McLaren's website contains Cedar Ridge's doctrinal statement. It includes a paragraph about Jesus Christ with no identification of his eternal deity, a reference to the Holy Spirit with no suggestion that he is God, and a declaration that, "God speaks to us in the Bible" without reference to its inspiration and inerrancy.[28] Regarding "unity", the statement reads, "Cedar Ridge recognises diversity among Christians in nonessential areas."[29] The paragraph gives no hint of what those nonessentials are. It is this lack of attention to detail which contributes to the view that the emerging church lacks discernment.

The emerging church deemphasises what it perceives to be "divisive" doctrine by emphasising the primacy of relationship over reasoned belief. This is characteristically postmodern. They also elevate God's (almost indiscriminate) love for mankind over his essential holiness and justice. By raising unity above truth, the emerging church creates an atmosphere where peace is the *summum bonum*, that is, the supreme good from which all others are derived.

The emerging church is essentially rooted in contemporary culture and this fact may be the cause of its own demise. Philosophies that are driven by culture are inexorably destined to disappear in time. As Os Guinness warned, "He who marries the spirit of the age soon becomes a widower."[30]

The advent of this movement raises questions about the nature of preaching in the emerging church. A writer identifying himself as "Pastor Pete" submitted questions regarding preaching in the emergent church on an internet blog:

> In the Reformed tradition, thanks to Karl Barth, we are often referring to the three-fold witness of the Word. That is, 1) the Word that took flesh in Jesus Christ, 2) that is witnessed to in Scripture, and 3) that is proclaimed in Word and Deed by the church. I'm particularly interested in your thoughts on the third (if there is a similar thread, please let me know). Specifically, what form will preaching take in the emergent church? In our tradition, the sermon has always taken centre stage. As a pastor who preaches every Sunday, I'm starting to become a little dissatisfied with the practice. I stress 'a little'. I look forward to doing it but the results are anti-climactic. I'm wandering, with the emergent church's leaning toward experience and relationship, if a guided communal conversation might replace a prepared, individual lecture? [31]

The responses to his questions indicate that new styles and structures in preaching are being tested. Graham Doel posted a response on the blog saying that he has experimented with conversational dialogue, congregational dialogue, creative story-telling and community topic selection.[32] Casey Tygrett, another participant on the blog, expresses frustration about current preaching:

> I realise even to use this term I'm dragging up a dead set of presuppositions, but in thinking about preaching, teaching or homiletizing, etc., there is for me a state of increasing frustration. Why don't people hear the truth in what I'm saying? Where is the response regarding their lives?

We trust in the spirit of truth to really get to the heart of things, but in the end the frustration of who undertakes to teach people about the Gospel is often intense and mysterious. Each talk, each exposition, crafted with hope and care is received as if it were a commencement address: 'Good sermon. Not too long.' People see it as my job—I see it as a matter of disseminating life or death challenges. There is only so long one can dive into and out of this pool before a mental and spiritual funk begins to develop.[33]

Dan Kimball, author of *The Emerging Church*, offers visions of modern preaching and postmodern preaching. In his view modern preaching is inadequate. He suggests that biblical terms like "gospel" and "Armageddon" need to be "deconstructed" and "redefined". In modern preaching the biblical text is communicated primarily with words whereas in postmodern preaching, "the scriptural message is communicated through a mix of words, visual arts, silence, testimony, and story and the preacher is a motivator who encourages people to learn from the Scriptures throughout the week."[34]

iv) Is something missing?

Capill maintains that the fundamental crisis in preaching is a "lack of spiritual vigour". He maintains that contemporary preaching is powerless, failing to convict sinners, convert the lost, sanctify the saints, produce deep and lasting change in people's lives, overwhelm people with sheer majesty, grandeur, excellence and beauty of God and his only son, Jesus Christ. He says, "it is the crisis of preaching that, for all its relevance, innovation or soundness is devoid of the power of the Holy Spirit."[35]

Martyn Lloyd-Jones expresses the same sentiment when appealing for something more than an intellectual presentation of biblical truth, "You are not simply imparting information, you are dealing with souls, you are dealing with pilgrims on the way to eternity, you are dealing with matters not only of life and death in this world, but with eternal destiny."[36] He goes on to say that the chief end of preaching is to give people a sense of the presence of God:

I can forgive a man for a bad sermon; I can forgive the preacher almost anything if he gives me a sense of God, if he gives me something for my soul…if he gives me some dim glimpse of the Glory of God, the love of Christ, my Saviour, and the magnificence of the gospel.[37]

However, a revolution in thinking has begun to emerge within the church. Pews are no longer filled with expectant congregations simply waiting to hear the preacher stand up and declare, "Thus says the Lord".

Instead, congregations are questioning what they see as the preacher's "opinion", without hesitating to offer their own.

Graham Johnston has correctly pointed out that, "What proved effective in communicating the gospel to a modern audience may not work in a postmodern culture."[38] In the modern world preachers had two options. Firstly, they could proclaim the Word of God with the knowledge that their listeners loved God and loved his Word. Secondly, they could take an apologetic approach and defend the Bible evidentially. These approaches are less likely to appeal to a postmodern congregation. Postmoderns tend to be far more sceptical, and less likely to be moved by apologetic arguments. The preacher will have to do more with this generation than with the previous one.

Postmodernism is now a reality in the pew. Congregation members are not, necessarily quoting Rorty, Foucault or Derrida, but they are espousing and embodying postmodern views, even if they have never been trained in postmodern philosophy. In the past, the preacher could stand in the pulpit and declare with unbridled authority, the truths of the Word of God. Now the preacher is viewed with suspicion by those who think he is trying to advance his own opinions and force them on others. There are people in the pews who do not believe there is such a thing as absolute truth. A survey was conducted at a large university in the USA where twenty students were asked if there is any such thing as absolute truth, "truth that is true across all times and cultures for all people". All but one of the students answered along the lines of: "truth is whatever you believe". "There is no absolute truth". "If there was such a thing as absolute truth how could we know what it is?" "People who believe in absolute truth are dangerous." The only exception was an evangelical Christian who said absolute truth was found in Jesus.[39] The signs point to a population that will increasingly question everything and not permit any possibility of absolutes. The challenge for the contemporary preacher is to reach postmodernists with the truth of the gospel. In the process of leading people to faith, wholeness and maturity in Christ they will also need to preach regularly to people who are influenced by a postmodern way of thinking.

v) Theological theories and preaching models: an overview

Preaching theory has been continuously developing from the first-century to the twenty-first century. New insights and emphases have influenced the church's understanding of the nature and role of the homiletic task so that in the contemporary context there is a wide spectrum of opinion on this matter. Gerrit Immink says, "Contemporary Homiletics shows a diversity of insights and operates from various presuppositions."[40] Even within specific denominations there is no consistent model and the intention and methodology varies. There are those who champion expository preaching and others who prefer narrative and topical styles of preaching.

In the last decades of the twentieth-century, North American homiletics was dominated by what has been called, "New Homiletics". During the first years of the new millennium, the emphasis has been moving further away from the modernist logos to postmodern poetics. In the Western European context, homiletics took an empirical turn following a heyday of kerygmatic theology. Karl Barth, Rudolph Bultmann and C. H. Dodd had understood preaching primarily as an encounter with God's redemptive presence, albeit in different ways.

The movement now is toward the process of understanding. How do the listeners engage in the process of understanding? The hearer of the sermon is seen as an active participant in the preaching process.[41] There is an increasing tendency to view preaching as a form of art. Vos, for example, says that the homiletician, "is to craft a sermon with care and make it a work of art".[42] Recent homiletical theories emphasise that texts can be understood in many different ways, that hearers provide their own interpretations and that imagination and metaphorical language are needed in order to represent the divine mystery.[43]

vi) Developments around the kerygmatic theory

Kerygma (Greek: κήρυγμα, kérugma) is the word used in the New Testament for preaching (see Luke 4:18-19, Romans 10:14 and Matthew 3:1). It is related to the Greek verb κηρύσσω (kērússō), to cry or proclaim as a herald, and means proclamation, announcement, or preaching. Davis argues that preaching in the New Testament takes the characteristic form of, "official announcement, proclamation of God's action and offer, by the mouth of a chosen messenger."[44] Proclamation is presented as a promise. It consists of promises made by God, promises of forgiveness and help, of liberation and joy, of hope and glory.[45] It may be surprising that the word "evangelism" does not appear in the Bible. However, "evangelists" are referred to three times (Acts 21:8, Ephesians 4:11 and 2 Timothy 4:5). The verb *euaggelizein* (to "evangelise'") occurs frequently; and the related noun *euaggelion* (gospel) appears frequently throughout the New Testament. The word *euaggelizein* means, "to communicate good news concerning something (in the New Testament a particular reference to the gospel message about Jesus)."[46] It expresses the good news of God's redemptive action in Jesus Christ. But Davis adds that the ministry of the Word is not derived from this concept alone. In the New Testament, teaching and exhortation are the legitimate forms of speech, "*Kerygma* points to God's decisive acts in Christ and calls for faith and repentance. Teaching and exhortation focus on the need in the community of faith to grow in knowledge, faith and obedience."[47]

The herald model is the preferred way of preaching by those who hold to a Word-theology. In his early days, Barth held that the church had forgotten to read the Word of God as God's Word. He was concerned that preaching had turned into a kind of religious discourse, a reflection of human needs and religious desires. He placed a strong emphasis on the otherness of God. He stated that, "The Gospel proclaims a God utterly distinct from men. Salvation comes to them from him, and because they are, as men, incapable of knowing him, they have no right to claim anything from him."[48] Therefore, in preaching, people are confronted with a critical and salvific Word of God, a Word that transforms.[49] The herald model reinforces that personal experiences, personal opinions, and colourful anecdotes are not truly important in the act of preaching.[50] Instead the divine-human encounter in Jesus Christ is to be re-presented. Preaching has to serve the Word of God, i.e. Jesus Christ as the act of God. For that reason preaching is the exposition of Scripture. Consequently Immink says:

> Our subjective experience or subjective interpretation is de-emphasised in the act of preaching. Instead, preaching is sacramental. It is a human speech act through which God's salvific action is re-presented, not in the sense that we can domesticate God, but rather that God can create the Christ event to be performed in our midst. Preaching is a kerygmatic event, not an expression of human consciousness.[51]

Bloesch questions the sad state of the sermon:

> Equally deplorable is the state of the sermon, which in historic Protestantism was considered the primary means of grace. Our preaching may appeal to the Bible, but that appeal is often more cultural than biblical. We interpret the Bible through the lens of our own experience or our particular religious tradition. We do not allow for the fact that the Spirit speaking to us through the Bible may call our traditions and our theologies into question. The surest evidence that Protestantism has abandoned its glorious heritage---of being not only a reformed church but a constantly reforming church---is the demise of kerygmatic preaching, preaching that consists in retelling the story of God's gift of salvation in Jesus Christ.

Ministers may preach from the Bible, but this does not guarantee that they are preaching the Word of God. Their sermons are didactic more than kerygmatic, more centred on moral concerns than on the gospel.[52]

Lischer advocates the kerygmatic approach in a more moderate form. He says that: "because it is God who speaks and the Holy Spirit who attends the Word, those who preach, teach and give testimony do so with the assurance that the Word's effective power is not diminished."[53] Long defines preaching as, "bearing witness" and Bartow emphasises the performance dimension of the kerygmatic model:[54]

And if the divine self-disclosure in Jesus Christ is the primary locus of performative action for practical theology...it is imperative that we attend to that self-disclosure with all the varied means appropriate to it...The Word of God is face to face, oral-aural situated, and suasory discourse. It is not a dead letter...It is an event of *action divinia* (God's self-performance). It is in fact God's human speech.[55]

The gospel here is primarily understood as an event of the divine self-performance. That self-performance is enacted again in preaching in the *homo performans*, where the divine action is encountered.[56] Preachers are not referring to the imaginations of their hearts, they testify to the divine self-performance. Language, therefore, does not have an expressive function, but instead it is relational and depicts reality. What it evokes is not merely knowledge or emotion, but instead human action brought about by the enactment of God's self-disclosure in preaching.[57]

A specific form of narrative kerygmatic homiletics has been developed in the Yale school of theology. It aims at overcoming the old liberal experiential-expressive model of religious communication by preaching a cultural linguistic-alternative. The old subjective approach is rejected, mainly because it locates religion in the pre-reflective depth of the self. In the old model faith is primarily a subjective experience and becomes discursive when it is expressed in thought and language. In a cultural-linguistic outlook religion is viewed as a kind of cultural or linguistic framework that shapes the entirety of life and thought.[58] Language and culture are *a-priori* and religion is a communal phenomenon that shapes subjectivity. The outer has priority over the inner and consequently religion is an external world that shapes the self and its world.[59]

Lowry introduced strategies for narrative sermons and holds the view that evoking an experience is the purpose of preaching. Yet there is an explicit kerygmatic moment in his theory of preaching. He distinguishes between preaching as a task and preaching as a goal and introduces the term "proclaiming" to describe the goal, "Preaching I can do. I choose it: I prepare for it. Prayerfully I engage it, and I perform it. I do it Sunday next. Proclaiming the Word is what I hope will happen next Sunday. I will attempt my preparation strategy in such a way as to maximise the chance for it."[60] Lowry points out that the bridge between preaching and truly proclaiming is evocation, but understood as an encounter with God's salvific presence.[61]

Immink maintains that it is important to see that kerygmatic preaching is not only stimulated by the Barthian tradition, but also by Bultmann's theology. According to Bultmann preaching is personal address, summons, demand and promise, "The message of Jesus is an eschatological gospel– the proclamation that now the fulfilment of promise is at hand, that now the kingdom of God begins."[62]

vii) The growing importance of the listener

One of the most fundamental characteristics of homiletical discourse in the second half of the twentieth century is the attention to the hearer.[63] It is necessary for the preacher to understand the world of the congregation. This requires more than the study of the Bible and commentaries but a penetration into the world of the congregation. Long states that the preacher must approach the text as a representative of the congregation, "We have been immersed in the lives of these people to whom we will speak, which is another way of saying that, symbolically at least we rise to the pulpit from the pew."[64]

This contributed to the development of hearer-centred models in homiletics. It was not that the kerygmatic theologians overlooked the listener, but their concern was primarily theological and epistemological in nature.

viii) The new homiletic

The dominant paradigm in the last quarter of the twentieth-century was the new homiletic. This movement can be labelled in different ways: poetic, narrative, imaginative, creative or transformational. One of the leading principles in preaching is that preaching must be understood as an event-in-time. The purpose of this kind of preaching is not to transmit cognitions but to facilitate an event to be experienced.[65] Good preaching does not seek to win consent to a truth claim, but evokes experience. An evaluation of the sermon is based on the question, what happened in this sermon.

Fred Craddock raises the practice of inductive preaching and he postulates three conditions which are necessary for inductive preaching:

> First, particular concrete experiences (of the listener and the preacher) are ingredient to the sermon...On the basis of these...conclusions are reached, new perspectives are gained, decisions made. The second...respects the hearer[s] right to participate...and arrive at a conclusion that is his own...This leads to a third and final comment about the inductive method and the role of the listener: the listener completes the sermon...What is suggested is that the participation of the hearer is essential...in the completion of the thought, movement and decision making within the sermon itself. The process calls for an incompleteness...in the sermon. It requires of the preacher that he resist the temptation to tyranny of ideas rather than democratic sharing...[66]

Induction begins with the particulars of life experience and points toward principles, concepts and conclusions.[67] In a later work Lewis and Lewis describe inductive preaching as, "laying out the evidence, the examples, the illustrations and postpone the declarations and assertions until the listeners have a chance to weigh the evidence, think through the implications and then come to the conclusion with the preacher at the end of the sermon."[68]

Another aspect of the New Homiletic is the use of creativity and imagination. Imagination is understood as a rule-governed form of invention. It has to do with inspiration and creativity.[69]

A good summary of more recent new directions in homiletics is found in Lucy Atkinson Rose's *Sharing the Word*. She favours a conversational model in which, "the preacher and the congregation gather symbolically at a round table without head or foot, where the labels like clergy and laity disappear and where believing or wanting to believe is all that matters."[70] All forms of hierarchy must be abandoned: the preacher is not an authority figure; there is no absolute or objective standard and no propositional truth. All present have a contribution in a partnership between the preacher and the congregation.[71]

Vos says, "The choice of the type of sermon has a communicative value and is a road along which the preacher and the congregation can travel."[72] As mentioned already, the preacher has responsibility for leading people to faith, wholeness and maturity in Christ.[73] It is his job to inspire listeners to a greater vitality of faith and a deeper and richer encounter with God in worship. But primarily the teacher is responsible for exposing people to the glory of God.

ix) Narrative preaching

The narrative preaching model is not entirely new. In the Bible there is what Walter Brueggermann[74] has called "primal narratives" such as Exodus. It was also prevalent in synagogue preaching, where preachers engaged in at least two distinct forms of proclamation: *halakah* (the way) and *haggadah* (story). *Halakah* involves applying the legal provisions of the Torah to new circumstances, while *haggadic* preaching weaves the hearer's circumstances into the biblical narratives.[75]

Narrative preaching is being promoted as a primary sermon form in the twenty-first century. It is argued by Davis that if only one-tenth of the gospel is exposition and nine-tenths of it narrative then why do: "perceptual sermons roar on, entirely out of sync with the Bible's narrative model?"[76]

In seeking to understand what narrative preaching is, it needs to be distinguished from story telling. Long defines a story as a series of events that have a beginning, a middle and an end.[77] These elements of time, says Pieterse, are "linked by logical relationships, by a casual relationship" or as suggested by Schlafer, "by the dynamics between narrative, images and arguments."[78] As Buttrick points out, however, the report of chronological events cannot be considered a narrative.[79] Stories may give identity or even prove a point or share ideas, whereas preaching in narrative form, transforms identity, because it places the story within the bigger context of God's story.[80] Although one cannot predict the effects of a sermon, the power of narrative is that it invites people to identify with a character in the narrative. Schlafer explains, "If a point of identification can be established with characters who are engaged in realistic interaction, there is the possibility that such an identification can have the effect of reshaping the life stories of those who hear the story in the sermon."[81]

Well told narratives draw the listener to the place where the listener identifies with the people in the story. Some characters are preferred above others but as the listener identifies with the trials and tribulations, the joys and loves of the characters, the listener develops a solidarity with them that enables him to say, "I like that" or "I wish I could be like that" or "I do not wish to be like that".[82] Or as Miller says, "What must I do?"[83]

Although the story captures the attention of the listener, instantaneous change cannot be guaranteed. Pieterse argues that the "single life-changing factor in Christian narratives is the life, death and resurrection of Jesus Christ"; therefore claiming that all preaching should be Christ-centred.[84]

Some see the narrative sermon to be the re-telling of the biblical story. Others understand narrative preaching to include a story about life that explains biblical truths. Illustrations, often used to confirm an expository sermon, as well as poetic language, the life story of the individual and authentic experiences are also considered by some to be narrative. Lowry defines narrative preaching in such broad terms that he regards each sermon, "that moves from opening disequilibrium through escalation of conflict to surprising reversal to closing denouement" as a narrative sermon whether it contains a story or not.[85]

The narrative sermon according to Calvin Miller is not a simple matter of using stories and illustrations to make the sermon interesting, instructive or challenging:

> The narrative sermon, rather than containing stories, is a story which, from the outset to conclusion, binds the entire sermon to a single plot as theme. Here and there sub-plots, separate illustrations or precepts may punctuate or ornament the narrative, but the theme narrative stays in force all the way through—from the sermon's 'once-upon-a-time' until its 'happy ever after'.[86]

According to Miller narrative preaching has a number of advantages.[87] It forces hearers to pay attention to more than the three point sermon form. It manoeuvres a story to suit the whole congregations privatised needs. Each member of the congregation applies the story to his situation to arrive at the best individual application. Vos maintains, "the main advantage of the story as a sermon is that it can be interesting, that it carries the listener along with it."[88]

x) Topical preaching

In a broad sense topical preaching takes place when the preacher:

> …is free to choose a text from the Bible rather than preach on a periscope assigned by the lectionary; when the preacher has an idea and then searches for a biblical text (or texts) treating the idea; even when the preacher writes on an assigned text but feels free to develop the sermon without rigid adherence to the structure of the text and without the compulsion to deal fully with every verse, phrase, or word in that text.[89]

There are others who define topical preaching more specifically. Caemmerer defines the topical sermon in terms of approach.[90] He sees the topical sermon beginning with a theme and goal in the mind of the preacher. It is the preaching on a subject which the preacher has begun to develop before he turns to a text to define it. Or it can be said that it is "need orientated rather than tradition orientated".[91]

Ronald J. Allen says that he is committed to the, "expository sermon being the life blood of the church" but argues for the use and value of the topical sermon on topics where the Bible is not explicitly clear.[92] He defines the topical sermon as interpreting a topic, "in the light of the gospel but without originating or centring on the exposition of a biblical text or theme." He goes on to define a topic as a need, an issue or a situation which is important to the congregation, which calls for interpretation from the perspective of the gospel itself than from the standpoint of the exposition of a particular passage from the Bible.

John A. Broadus defines the topical sermon mainly in terms of the development of the sermon's structure, "Topical sermons are those in which the divisions are derived from the subject. The topic may be derived from the text, but the divisions come from the subject."[93] The starting point here is the text and not the preacher's idea. The text may even suggest the topic but what makes the sermon topical is that the sermon outline is developed in terms of headings natural to the topic rather than those indicated by the text.[94]

There are at least three elements that Rossow identifies as essential for topical preaching. First, the selected topic must be a biblical topic, or, if not that, at least a topic treated and resolved from a biblical perspective. He insists that the sermon topic must, "ultimately have a 'Thus says the Lord' quality to it." In other words the authority of the scriptures must be clear.[95]

Second, in spite of the preacher developing his theme in his own individual way and possibly not dealing with all aspects of the text, "there must be considerable congruence between the content of the sermon and the content of the text."[96] When a preacher embarks on the task of topical preaching, he must not distort or disregard the meaning of the biblical text.

Third, the topical sermon must communicate the gospel, "the good news of God's saving and sanctifying help through the life, death and resurrection of Jesus Christ, the Son of God."[97] The gospel must be seen as paramount, the principal ingredient, as the major reason why the sermon was preached at all.

xi) Advantages of topical preaching

Various advantages of topical preaching have been identified. Firstly, it is more focused on the needs of the hearer and can be more rewarding. The preacher's mind is, therefore, trained in logical analysis.[98] Secondly the preacher may consult individuals or groups in the congregation for their input as to choice of sermon topics and/or texts, thereby increasing the likelihood of sermons being relevant to individual and congregational needs.[99] The topical sermon encourages the preacher and the congregation to be able to describe contemporary issues and situations.

xii) Expository preaching and a scene from Nehemiah

A dramatic scene recorded in Nehemiah gives an excellent illustration of the nature of expository preaching. It is a scene described by Larsen and Dahlen as, "not a spontaneous gathering but well planned and strategically arranged."

> And all the people gathered as one man into the square before the Water Gate. And they told Ezra the scribe to bring the Book of the Law of Moses that the LORD had commanded Israel. So Ezra the priest brought the Law before the assembly, both men and women and all who could understand what they heard, on the first day of the seventh month. And he read from it facing the square before the Water Gate from early morning until midday, in the presence of the men and the women and those who could understand. And the ears of all the people were attentive to the Book of the Law. And Ezra the scribe stood on a wooden platform that they had made for the purpose...And Ezra opened the book in the sight of all the people, for he was above all the people, and as he opened it all the people stood. And Ezra blessed the LORD, the great God, and all the people answered, "Amen, Amen," lifting up their hands. And they bowed their heads and worshiped the LORD with their faces to the ground...the Levites, helped the people to understand the Law, while the people remained in their places. They read from the book, from the Law of God, clearly, and they gave the sense, so that the people understood the reading.[100]

Raymond Brown, commenting on this passage, says, "the distinctive characteristics of this meeting for biblical exposition are strikingly relevant...Western materialistic culture has become increasingly indifferent to the Bible."[101] Brueggemann, commenting on Nehemiah, suggests that, "particular attention be paid to the remarkable cluster of materials in chapters 8-10...The text narrates a determinative act...that marks the community of Judaism as the people of the book-cum-interpretation."[102]

Expository preaching seeks to follow the pattern established by Ezra and his associates. Those men read God's book and explained it and they did so in such a way that the people understood the implications.[103] Expository preaching is Bible-centred. That means handling the text, "in such a way that its real and essential meaning as it existed in the mind of the particular Bible writer as it exists in the light of the over-all context of

Scripture is made plain and applied to the present-day needs of the hearers."[104] The text of Scripture must be explained in such a way that people understand what God is saying to them.[105] Expository preaching creates an expectation among hearers to hear what it is that God is saying. Calvin expresses this:

> It is certain that if we come to church we shall not hear only a mortal man speaking but we shall feel (even by his secret power) that God is speaking to our souls, that he is the teacher. He so touches us that the human voice enters into us and so profits us that we are refreshed and nourished by it. God calls us to him as if he had his mouth open and we saw him there in person.[106]

xiii) Key principles of expository preaching

Expository preaching always begins with the text. That does not mean that every sermon will begin with the phrase, "please turn in your Bible to…" But it does mean that even when one begins by referring to some current event or the lyric of a contemporary song, it is the text of Scripture that establishes the agenda for the sermon. The expositor does not start with a private idea, instead he begins with Scripture itself and allows the verses under consideration to establish and frame the content of the sermon.[107] The congregation should be able to see that it is from the text of Scripture that the preacher derives truths put forth in the sermon.[108] This is a basic principle put succinctly in *The Directory for the Public Worship of God*, written in 1645:

> It is presupposed (according to the rules for ordination) that the minister of Christ is in some good measure gifted for so weighty a service, by his skill in the original languages, and in such arts and sciences as are handmaids unto divinity; by his knowledge in the whole body of theology, but most of all in the holy scriptures.[109]

When raising an issue from a text, preachers, according to the *Confession of Faith* are to ensure that, "it be a truth contained in or grounded on that text." And "that the hearers may discern how God teacheth it from thence."[110] Those who preach must ensure that their efforts lead to the listeners understanding their Bibles. This conviction led those involved in the English Reformation to include in their first book on homiletics the clear instruction, "The Word of God alone is to be preached, in its perfection and inner consistency. Scripture is the exclusive subject of preaching, the only field in which the preacher is to labour."[111]

That is why John Stott says, "It is our conviction that all true Christian preaching is expository preaching."[112]

It is inaccurate, therefore, to think of expository preaching merely as a style chosen from a list (narrative, topical, devotional, evangelistic, apologetic, prophetic or expository). Roy Clements confirms this:

> Expository preaching is not a matter of style at all. In fact the determinative step which decides whether a sermon is going to be expository or not takes place, in my view, before a single word has been actually written or spoken. First and foremost the adjective 'expository' describes the method by which the preacher decides what to say, not how to say it.[113]

The task of the expositor goes beyond a running commentary on a passage or even a succession of word studies loosely held together by a few illustrations. It goes beyond the discovery and declaration of the central doctrine found in the passage.

In preaching the aim must be to let the text speak. As Von Rad instructed young preachers, "every text wants to speak for itself".[114] The preacher should not only try to find out what the text means but he should also ask, "What is the passage trying to do?"[115] In the words of Gerhard Ebeling, "the sermon is the execution of the text...it is the proclamation of what the text has proclaimed."[116] The text provides both information and proclamation and as the Bible is read and preached God speaks to us today.[117]

In expository preaching, the preacher stands between two worlds. Expository preaching seeks to fuse the two horizons of the biblical text and the contemporary world. Stott argues that it is possible to preach exegetically and yet fail to answer the "so what?" in the listener's mind.[118] Ezra's hearers would not have begun construction on the booths if he had failed to establish the link between the text and the times. True exposition must have some prophetic dimension that leaves the listener in no doubt that what he has heard is a living word from God and creates in him at least the sneaking suspicion that the author knows him. The preacher's task is to declare what God has said, explain the meaning and establish the implications so that no one will mistake its relevance. Stott says, "Biblical and theological studies do not of themselves make for good preaching. They are indispensable. But unless they are supplemented by contemporary studies, they can keep us disastrously isolated on one side of the cultural chasm."[119] David Read commends the need for study but goes on to say, "...that theology-cushioned, isolated study is a lethal chamber, and it is a dead word that is carried out along the corridor...not the living Word spoken as it must be, from the heart and from life to life."[120] So it is necessary for the preacher to understand the world of the congregation and this requires more than study of the Bible and commentaries. It necessitates a penetration into the world of the congregation.

Good expository preaching can show relevance, as it encourages the listener to understand why a first-century letter to a church in Corinth, say, is relevant to a twenty-first century congregation living in London. The horizons of the biblical text and the contemporary world should fuse in such a way that the listeners are learning by example how to integrate the Bible with their own experience. Listeners face the twin dangers of assuming either what they have just heard is totally unrelated to where they are living or that it is immediately applicable, that it is "just for them".[121] Vos says:

> The preacher has to place himself in the text's situation (horizon), whilst being true to one's own situation (horizon). In the hermeneutical interaction that follows (putting one's prejudices as questions and listening to the text's answers to these questions) the preacher's horizon is broadened.[122]

Vos concludes, "Speaking and listening happens in dialogues. A dialogue with the biblical text can occur where there is critical exegetical analysis and attentive listening on the part of the preacher."[123]

Expository preaching depends on the work of the Holy Spirit. Azurdia claims that:

> The greatest impediment to the advancement of the gospel is the attempt of the church of Jesus Christ to do the work of God apart from the truth and power of the Spirit of God. Like the disciples, preachers are powerless, in and of themselves, to accomplish the 'greater works'. The declaration of Jesus in John 15:15 remains true to this day: "Apart from me you can do nothing".[124]

Pieterse confirms this by saying that people can only hear the living Word in preaching through the work of the Holy Spirit.[125] Hughes argues that belief in the power of the Holy Spirit and dependence on that power should not "give us licence to be mediocre communicators."[126] The same warning is given (rather sardonically) by Spurgeon to preachers who fail to employ effective homiletic techniques:

> There are some preachers who care very little whether they are attended to or not, so long as they can hold on through the allotted time it is of very small importance to them whether their people hear from eternity, or hear

in vain: the sooner such ministers sleep in the churchyard and preach by the verse on their gravestone the better.[127]

While the Holy Spirit can do anything he wants, "he has called us to preach the word and to preach it clearly, to preach it accurately and to preach to communicate the content of the gospel."[128]

xiv) The advantages of expository preaching

Liefeld lists a number of advantages from the preacher's point of view. These may be summarised as follows.[129] The preacher can be more confident of preaching God's will when preaching the Word of God. True exposition increases that confidence and the sense of authority that grows out of it. In expository preaching the preacher can confine himself to biblical truth and minimise subjectivism. By using this model the preacher in preaching through the Bible is more likely to proclaim the "whole counsel of God" rather than using favourite parts of Scripture. Begg agrees, "expository preaching prevents the preacher from avoiding difficult passages or from dwelling on favourite texts."[130] Liefeld points out that the context of the passage usually includes its own application. The preacher therefore gets directions as to how the passage should be applied in the present day. Scripture often provides a pattern that reveals the inner thoughts and feelings of the author. This can provide excellent suggestions for sermon outlines. Expository preaching sets limits, as explained by John Stott, "it restricts us to the scriptural text", and does not allow us to invent our own message.[131] One of the main advantages of expository preaching is that the preacher will never be lost for a subject for his sermon, since few preachers have ever preached through the entire Bible in their lifetime. Through expository preaching the preacher walks in the path of the original writer and there is less of a tendency for the preacher to preach his own opinion or the philosophy of the age.[132]

Begg adds some important advantages of expository preaching by pointing out that it gives glory to God, which ought to be the ultimate end of all spiritual activity.[133] He points out that since expository preaching begins with the text of Scripture, it starts with God and is in itself an act of worship, for it is a declaration of the mighty acts of God. It establishes the focus of the people upon God and his glory before any consideration of man and his need. In this way, the place of preaching is affirmed not on the grounds of personal interest but because it pleases God. According to Begg, a congregation that has accepted this and is beginning to learn the implications of it, will be markedly different from the one in which sermons constantly find their origin in the felt needs of the people.

Expository preaching makes the preacher study God's Word. The preacher who commits himself to the expository approach will become a student of Scripture. The first heart God's Word needs to reach is that of the preacher. John Owen spoke of this necessity for the preacher to experience the power of truth in his own soul, "A man only preaches a sermon well to others if he has first preached it to himself. If he does not thrive on the 'food' he prepares, he will not be skilled at making it appetizing for others. If the Word does not dwell with power in us, it will not pass on power from us."[134]

CHAPTER FOUR

INDUCTIVE AND DEDUCTIVE MODES
OF PREACHING

The previous chapter presents an overview and analysis of the different forms of preaching. In this final chapter, in the light of what has been said so far, the question remains of what the most appropriate model for communicating with postmoderns may be.

Each model seems to present good reasons for usage, whether narrative, topical or expository preaching. However, the case for expository preaching seems compelling for every generation from the first-century to the twenty-first century, irrespective of philosophy or culture and this presents new challenges in contemporary culture where a significant paradigm shift has occurred.

Postmodernism is not just a philosophical approach taken by academicians, it is emerging as a popular worldview in contemporary culture and it does not appear to be a passing fad. Even the attitudes of "church people" have been shaped by this paradigm shift and preachers who fail to take this seriously may find themselves faced with people who consider their preaching to be totally irrelevant.

i) Approaches toward connecting with postmoderns

The response to the challenge of postmodernism has taken on a number of different approaches. The goal of preaching has always involved bridging the gap between the ancient world of the biblical text and the contemporary culture. How that gap is bridged without sacrificing revelation or relevance is one of the greatest challenges in the contemporary context. On the one hand the significance of revelation could be watered down so as to avoid criticism from the contemporary hearers, or the significance of the philosophical approach of the contemporary hearers could be diminished. Either of these approaches may serve one side of the bridge well, but neither will meet the goal of bridging the gap and faithfully preserving both *revelation* and *relevance*.

As Graham Johnston has said, "The task is to engage people anew, with a fresh voice so that even in this millennium, the gospel will remain the good news."[1] But how can that be done since the world has become so much more complicated since the advent of postmodernism? Millard Erickson has provided a helpful classification of the varied approaches to connecting with postmoderns, "Can deconstructed horses even be led to water?"[2] There are three elements in this question that bear explanation: the deconstructed horses represent the postmodern audiences, the water represents the message, the device that leads them to the water, say a rope, represents the method of bringing them to the message.

A variety of possible responses are possible. First, there are two negative responses, "no, deconstructed horses cannot be led to water, so ignore them and go after other horses." In other words, postmoderns cannot be reached, so they should be ignored and attention should be focused on those who have not adopted postmodern views. Obviously this is an approach that some ministers will take either out of frustration or lack of understanding. That does not seem to be a viable option. Another negative approach is to say, "no, postmoderns cannot be reached, but if one ignores them and keeps preaching maybe they'll come around some day". That approach has the same problems as the first, but may at least leave the door open for the minister to continue appealing to postmoderns. But that still leaves those deconstructed horses thirsty.

There are several positive responses to this question that bear examination. Another analogy could be, "yes, the deconstructed horses can be led to water, but one has to deconstruct the water". This approach admits the postmoderns have accepted certain tenets of postmodernism and therefore the message needs to be postmodernized. This would involve reframing Christian theology by eliminating the following: the objectivity of reality, the correspondence theory of truth, metanarratives and objective morality, to name a few. This is the approach adopted by Mark Taylor, Middleton and Walsh and Stanley Grenz. Mark Taylor, following the tradition of Jacques Derrida, "eludes the concept of truth altogether in favour of language sport." He calls his theology "a/theology" and freely admits that his theology is, "erratic or even erroneous" and therefore never fixed in meaning but always in transition.[3] Middleton and Walsh read the Scriptures through a postmodern lens and discover new dimensions in the biblical text of which they were previously unaware.[4] Their readings may be in step with postmodernism but appear to sacrifice too much for the sake of relevance. Stanley Grenz calls for a re-visioning of evangelical theology and suggests that, "efforts to establish the role of Scripture in Christian theology are 'ultimately unnecessary.'"[5] The obvious problem with this approach is that it gives up too much and in the process leaves too much out. The goal in reaching postmoderns is not to open dialogue, though that may be an important first step. The goal is ultimately transformation, and sacrificing revelation will not achieve that goal.

The second positive response is, in the terms of another analogy, "yes one can lead the deconstructed horses to water, but first the rope must be deconstructed." This response suggests that in order to reach postmoderns, preaching style must be thoroughly changed. This approach is better than the first approach because it does not sacrifice the message, at least in theory.

One of the trends of the last four decades has been a move toward narrative theology, a narrative hermeneutic and a narrative homiletic. This trend in new homiletics was birthed primarily as a reaction against deductive, propositional preaching. Contemporary advocates are saying that, "propositional preaching is no longer a viable method of communicating with today's postmodern audience."[6] Fred Craddock is considered by many to have launched the movement. In his monograph, *As One Without Authority*, he argued that the goal of preaching is not to communicate information, but to produce an experience in the hearers, so that they see the world from a gospel perspective.[7] In some cases this approach has resulted in adopting a narrative hermeneutic that reduces Scripture to a text which can only produce revelation / illumination when it is properly read or heard. In other words, some have suggested, with Brunner, that the Bible *becomes* the Word of God when it is properly proclaimed.

It is true that some have utterly rejected propositional truth in order to make the message more palatable. Nevertheless, it is also possible to blend a narrative methodology harmoniously with propositional truth. The latter version seems more promising in satisfying the twofold goal of retaining both revelation and relevance.

A third response to the question, "can deconstructed horses even be led to water?" is "yes, but the horse is not really deconstructed".[8] This approach says that though they think they are deconstructed, in fact they are not. This position is adopted by David Wells, who is critical of evangelical collusion with modernity, but assumes that certain apologetic responses will still be effective with postmoderns. In some ways Thomas Oden takes this approach. He suggests that the phenomenon is not postmodernism but "ultramodernism" or "hypermodernism". In other words these are moderns who have taken modernism to another level.[9]

It could be argued that at least among the authors who accept the label "postmodern", they exhibit a strong tendency toward repudiation of some aspects of modernism. The depth of philosophical scepticism or suspicion that is inherent in postmodernism requires more from preachers than a casual nod. If this shift is not taken seriously, the Christian voice may become irrelevant and lack any opportunity for reaching the coming generations.

It is interesting that these three approaches—change the message, change the method and reject the problem—are approaches that the church used when faced with the challenge of modernism. Liberalism adopted the first two, and fundamentalism, at least to some degree, adopted the third. It seems appropriate that the church should learn from history, especially considering the fact that a Christian response took so long to be formulated. Perhaps that is why so many are reluctant to give up on modernist apologetics because it has finally been nailed down and now the church is faced with a new challenge.

There is a fourth approach to this question and that is to first deconstruct the horse.[10] This approach suggests taking up the challenge of postmodernism, and either utilising their own tools of deconstruction, or some other arguments, to help to enable it to assume a more favourable and receptive position. Erickson has pointed out that Francis Schaeffer took this approach even before the term postmodern was being used by Christians. He saw the rejection of truth and the "line of despair" long before many others in the evangelical world became aware of what was happening in contemporary culture. One of his goals at L'Abri was to help young philosophers see where their thinking was taking them and help them reject a turn toward nihilism and despair and accept instead the message of hope in the gospel.[11] This is a valid enterprise and one of the more promising approaches to meeting the challenge of postmodernism. It may be difficult to utilise this approach from the pulpit but it has promise in various campus ministries.[12]

Another approach which cannot be overlooked is the position taken by Leonard Sweet. Using Erickson's analogy, he advocates "deconstructing the rope" calling on ministers to change the method they use for reaching postmoderns, but he suggests further that the ministers themselves need to be deconstructed. In *Carpe Manana* Sweet labels everyone born before 1962 as an "immigrant" and everyone born after 1962 as a "native".[13] This labelling has huge implications for ministry. It suggests that the younger, emerging generation is so steeped in postmodern ways of thinking that deconstructing them is unlikely and may be impossible. Sweet takes an assimilationist perspective and argues that they don't need deconstructing;

those who are "immigrants" need to learn to think more like them. In *Postmodern Pilgrims*, Sweet sets out to develop a plan for ministering to postmoderns, suggesting that:

> Ministry in the twenty-first century has more in common with the first-century than with the modern world that is collapsing all around us. *Postmodern Pilgrims* aims to demodernize the Christian consciousness and reshape its way of life according to a more biblical vision of life that is dawning with the coming of the postmodern era.[14]

Unlike some of the authors who have written about postmodernism, Sweet is positive and optimistic. He sees the church of the future reaching out with love to postmoderns and adapting methods and approaches to meet their needs. There is much in Sweet's position that is attractive. The main thesis of *Postmodern Pilgrims* is the development of a ministry model that he calls "EPIC". This is an acronym for *experiential, participatory, image-laden* and *connected*. With this approach he argues that the church can be "biblically absolute but culturally relative".[15]

One of Sweet's more salient points is his description of the sweeping changes that have come about as a result of the advent of the internet. Sweet argues that these elements, experiential, participatory, image-laden and connected, are what drive postmoderns to the internet world and they are essential to their way of viewing reality and apprehending truth. Therefore he urges churches in general and ministers in particular to take these elements seriously when developing programmes and preaching sermons aimed at reaching postmoderns.

According to Sweet, postmoderns actually think in completely new ways. He points out that the old way of thinking was more linear, the new way is non-linear or "loopy". He even argues that the changes in learning style are the reason so many children are prescribed Ritalin for Attention Deficit Disorder (A.D.D.). He quotes one teenager, who, while swallowing his Ritalin asked his mother, "Do you think they'll ever stop giving pills to kids who think in circles and not straight?"[16] Sweet explains this connection between linear and non-linear thinking:

> Linear competence is single-minded. The teacher occupies centre stage. It's 'skill and drill' stress memory retention, reduction meaning, and creation of an ordered worldview with cause and effect and beginning and ending. It's 'workplace' is the classroom. Nonlinear, digital competence is stacked. The student occupies centre stage. It stresses rapid hand-eye coordination, mental ability to make quick connections, the ability to organise information, skills at accessing rather than memorising

information, and puts a 'spin' on meaning rather than reduces it. It's
'workplace' is anywhere.[17]

Other writers have begun to use the term "abduction" for the way
postmoderns apprehend truth. It is neither by deduction nor induction, but
through a sense experience that existentially captures their imagination
and causes them to believe.[18] Sweet argues that postmoderns do not come
to church asking, "Is it true?" rather they come asking, "Is it real?" In
other words they are not looking for proof, they want an experience.[19] The
implications for this new way of thinking are the primary reasons Sweet
has made such sweeping suggestions for altering the way churches do
business in the postmodern world.

The Christian community will not reach this generation if it keeps
attacking it. One way of demonstrating genuine concern for postmoderns
is to take their unique needs seriously. There is a need to prioritise their
concerns when preparing sermons intended to reach them. Amy Mears and
Charles Bugg point out some of the unique needs of postmodern
audiences. They suggest five needs that are often overlooked and bear
special consideration in a postmodern context, "the need for acceptance,
the need for hope, the need for ecological awareness, the need for
inclusion, and the need for distinctiveness."[20] It is not surprising that
postmoderns have a need for acceptance and hope as these are needs for
all people. If their belief system is permeated by postmodern relativism,
preaching can provide them with an escape from the nihilism and
solipsism of postmodernity. Approaches to reaching them should reflect
the hope found in assurance through Jesus Christ.

The postmodern need for ecological awareness represents a more
difficult prospect. It is true, as Mears and Bugg have pointed out, that,
"Some evangelicals have viewed the so-called social gospel with
suspicion." And getting people saved has been a higher priority than,
"getting the world saved."[21] Recognising that, "this is our Father's world"
and God has granted "dominion" over the earth, Mears and Bugg suggest
that ministry to postmoderns should take into consideration this
postmodern concern. In some ways evangelical eschatology has eschewed
focus on the planet, recognising that God will create a "new Heaven and a
new Earth". But the ecological ethic of protecting and preserving the
planet does fit within the biblical mandate in Genesis and being sensitive
to this need in postmoderns may go a long way in ministering to them.

What postmoderns need to hear from the pulpit is a message of the
distinctiveness of Christianity. If the signal is sent that Christians are just
like everyone else with no distinction then there is a risk of establishing
what so many already believe, that Christianity is just hypocrisy. The

pulpit should ring with a call to be different from the world. In the 1960's the hippy culture latched on to this message in the "Jesus movement". What turned many of them away from the church was the pressure for them to conform by cutting their hair and abandoning their preference in music. The appeal to this generation must not replicate these mistakes but rather look beyond the outward trappings of contemporary expressions toward the inward distinctiveness found in Jesus.

The fifth need, Mears and Bugg point out is the need for inclusion.[22] Christians are guilty of using non-inclusive language. It would be helpful to translate some of the male dominant language of the Bible, for instance, so that it reflects or more openly represents both genders.[23]

In addition to these five needs there are other, epistemological needs. It was noted earlier that postmoderns employ a "hermeneutic of suspicion". They are suspicious of truth claims that, in their opinion, often harbour a hidden agenda of the privileged few or oppression of the marginalised. This suggests that in order to connect with postmoderns their need to evaluate truth claims must be taken seriously. The employment of lessons learned from deconstruction can be helpful in this regard.

It has been pointed out that postmodernists reject all metanarratives as explanations for reality because they are seen as too all-encompassing and oppressive. This suggests that postmoderns have a need to feel that their story is not left out by some over-arching scheme of reality. It must be demonstrated that the message of the Christian gospel is a story about all of humanity and not just about one culture, race or ethnicity. It will be necessary to jettison the jargon used in church in order to communicate effectively with postmoderns. In order to meet these epistemological needs it may be necessary to employ some of the methods utilised by missionaries in translating the gospel, in both linguistic and cultural terms. The cultural elements of Christianity are often assumed to be essential whereas they are particularistic social models borrowed from the secular world and baptised into the church. Unpacking these social and cultural elements may be the greatest tool in reaching postmodern audiences.

ii) A brief etymological analysis of preaching

What is the appropriate Christian response to the postmodern worldview? It is necessary to explore what it means to develop an effective apologetic in the contemporary situation. But first it will be helpful to define the terms of reference by clarifying what is meant by "preaching".

A brief inspection of the words to describe and define preaching in the New Testament reveals something of the nature of the undertaking.[24] The most common word translated into English as "preach" or "preaching" is κηρύσσω, (kerússō). This is used in 2 Timothy 4:2 where the apostle Paul instructs Timothy to, "preach the word". Timothy would have understood this command as invested with divine authority. Preaching was proclaiming or heralding the Word of God as a royal representative or ambassador.[25] The significance of this is that the preacher (messenger), the preaching act, the message itself and the king who sent it are all inextricably connected to each other. Fabarez says, "kērussō depicts an act that is always relevant, always important, and always powerful."[26]

Words of the same linguistic derivation are euvaggelizw (euaggellízō), καταγγελλω (kataggello), and αvvαγγελλω (anaggello). This family of words have their root in the word translated as "angel", a heavenly messenger sent by God to transmit a message. These cognate words imply, in addition to the literal or primary meaning, that the announcement is of great importance.[27] The word διδάσκω, (didásko), commonly translated as "to teach" is often connected to the words cited above and means more than just the transmission of information. Didasko is teaching with the purpose of initiating and sustaining transformation, not just the imparting and retention of information. This is evident in the "Great Commission", "Go therefore and make disciples of all nations, baptizing them in the name of the Father and of the Son and of the Holy Spirit, teaching them to observe all that I have commanded you. And behold, I am with you always, to the end of the age." (Matthew 28:19-20).

These words contribute to an understanding of preaching and teaching as authoritative, powerful and life-changing activity in the salvation and sanctification of people. Paul's instruction to Timothy contains several verbs that keep the objectives of preaching in sharp focus. In 2 Timothy 4:2 Paul clarifies what he means by "preach the word" when he adds; "reprove", "rebuke", and "exhort". The Greek word evlegcw (eléncho) translated "reprove" is used by Jesus in Matthew 18:15 to explain how to point out a brother's sin and cause him to alter his behaviour. Jesus said, "go and tell him his fault" (eléncho). The word translated as "rebuke" is εpitimaw (epitimáo), the second verb used by Paul in clarifying the nature and intention of preaching. Lexicographers interpret this word as speaking or warning, "in order to prevent an action or bring one to an end."[28] It is the word used to describe Christ's command to the wind and the waves to cease their activity (Matthew 8:26; Mark 4:39; Luke 8:24). The third word used by Paul to describe preaching is parakaleō and it is frequently translated as "exhort", "urge" or "beseech". This word can have a wider meaning in the New Testament but in this context it compliments the previous two verbs while conveying an intensity not communicated by them. This is evident in Paul's use of the word in 1 Timothy 1:3 when he urged παρεκαλεω (*parakaleō*) Timothy to remain in Ephesus and teach, in Ephesians 4:1 when he urges (*parakaleō*) Christians in Ephesus to live a life worthy of their calling, and in Romans 12:1 when Paul appeals (*parakaleō*) to the Roman Christians to offer themselves to God as living sacrifices. In every instance it is apparent that Paul desires and supposes that preaching should generate a noticeable alteration in the lives of those who hear and heed the message.

iii) The Holy Spirit: past and constant agent

The history of the early church reveals the power of preaching Christ. Preaching Christ in the power of the Holy Spirit was the effective means of reaching multitudes and signalled a significant and radical shift in religious thought. It was by this God-ordained means that the world was turned upside down.[29] Many writers today still believe in the relevance and efficacious merit of dynamic, Spirit-filled preaching. And some older works on preaching are being reprinted for the contemporary minister of Scripture. Much that is written today looks to the past for supporting argument.[30] William Sangster, for instance, argues that the preacher should reacquaint himself with what preaching has done in the history of the church and that such thoughts should instil a sense of the value of preaching and inspire the preacher to have confidence in this method of communication. He claims:

> When he thinks on all that God has done by preaching through the years—Gregory of Nazianzus, Chrysostom, Ambrose, Bernard of Clairvaux, Wycliffe, Edwards, Spurgeon, Hugh Price Hughes and tens of thousands of lesser known men—he will not wave it aside as 'sound and fury, signifying nothing'.[31]

Sangster says, that "Preaching is a constant agent of the divine power"[32] and that, "God uses it to change lives."[33]

Society has become increasingly secularised on the one hand and increasingly interested in alternative spiritualities on the other. This is evident in New-Age trends and a decrease in attendance at traditional Christian churches. Some might argue that the church survives by adapting itself to the prevailing culture but the corrective argument is that the church then loses its counter-cultural influence. However, to counter this argument some might say that the main Christian events, such as

Christmas and Easter, are evidence of how pagan festivals can be successfully integrated into the church and so the argument goes on. There is a decline in traditional Christian religion, and growth in alternative spiritualities, secularism and pluralism.

It seems that generations past had a higher regard for preaching than today's generation. This is not to say that there is little or no regard for preaching, rather to say that it is less widespread than it used to be. There are circles where preaching is held in high regard today but these circles have diminished. Certainly, looking back at the past there is ample evidence of that high regard for preaching. John Calvin said, "The office of teaching is committed to pastors for no other purpose than that God alone may be heard there."[34] Deitrich Bonhoeffer expressed the view that, "The sermon is not a discourse in which I develop my own thoughts; it is not my word but God's own word."[35]

David Hilborn has argued that contemporary evangelical leaders are saying that, "the expository age" has come to an end with the demise of the Enlightenment. He suggests that, "new methods of evangelism and new styles of worship must be developed if the church is not to suffer the fate of a maladapted dinosaur in the postmodern cultural environment which increasingly dominates the western world."[36] His view that preaching will take on a minor role in the days ahead seems short-sighted and pessimistic. There is danger that attempts to adapt to the prevailing culture will become syncretistic. It is true that as the landscape continues to shift toward postmodernism, preachers will have to adjust, but preaching will continue to have a role to play. It should be pointed out that congregations will not be entirely composed of postmoderns. For some the Enlightenment is a failed project but for others it is an incomplete project. There will still be moderns and pre-moderns occupying the pews for years to come. Evangelistic techniques which incorporate new insights into reaching postmoderns are currently being developed and a new environment does indeed call for new approaches to evangelism. However, preaching occupies a place in the church which extends beyond evangelism.

Don Bartel suggests that America is now a mission field and that the church's approach should be more like a "mission outpost strategy."[37] He urges adopting the policy of the Navigators by going out and reaching the un-churched world. Jimmy Long suggests the development of a "loving community". He quotes an InterVarsity staff member who defines a loving community as, "The greatest apologetic for Christianity is not a well-reasoned argument but a wildly loving community. Our Lord did not say they will know us by our truths, as important as that is; truth is very important, but they will know us by our love."[38] One could readily agree with both these approaches to evangelism. It seems appropriate to have a broad range of approaches to meet the complex needs of postmoderns but these do not necessarily need to exclude preaching. Preaching should not be abandoned as an outdated approach to reaching people and ministering to them. When the "mission outposts" and "loving communities" have reached postmoderns they will need some place to send them where they can grow as Christians and be equipped to reach back to their friends and neighbours outside the church. Postmodern issues regarding the way people think and apprehend truth will continue long after their conversion.

iv) Contemporary approaches to preaching

Arturo Azurdia offers some insights into some of the approaches that have become prevalent in contemporary culture. He cites two current methods that are relevant to this discussion: the use of psychology and the use of marketing strategy. Both of these, he argues, can be employed without the use of the Holy Spirit.[39] He points out that some preachers have abandoned Scripture and instead use psychology in their preaching. This approach begins with a need in the congregation and the preacher then searches through self-help books or psychology books for an answer to that need. The preacher develops a message and just before delivery inserts a Bible verse or two here and there to make the sermon seem biblical.

A second approach is the use of marketing strategies.[40] This approach again begins with a need in contemporary society and develops a strategy for meeting that need. These sermons usually provide a step-by-step approach to overcoming some problem in much the same way as a self-help book handles problems. In some ways this is preaching by polling. The preacher finds out what topics he should dwell on and what topics to avoid. Sermons on marriage and family are acceptable but sermons on sin, hell and judgement are avoided. This approach ultimately strips the Word of God of any truths that might turn people off. In a way, the preacher who adopts this strategy sacrifices *revelation* for the sake of *relevancy*.

Those who advocate these approaches argue that they work and as they produce the desired results they should, therefore, be employed. On the one hand there is a temptation to affirm these approaches because of their "success" whereas on the other hand there is a reluctance to endorse them because too much is being sacrificed for the sake of "results".

Tim Keller argues that preaching on moral issues must avoid two extremes, *pragmatism* and *moralism*.[41] In the pragmatic approach, preaching moral issues involves teaching people about the efficacy of being moral. For example sex outside marriage can lead to disease and ruined lives both emotionally and spiritually. The problem with this approach is that it ultimately breaks down. A person might use this approach for a while but then discover that sin can lead to short term happiness and that can become the highest good and therefore pragmatic. Keller says, "Christian morality is not true because it works; it works because it's true."[42]

The other approach is moralistic. This is preaching that says; "you should be good because God commands it" or "you should be moral because it's the right thing to do". The problem with this approach is that it could easily be confused with the teachings of almost any other religious tradition. What sets Christianity, in terms of morality, apart from Buddhism, Hinduism or Islam, is grace. The Christian ethic is not meritorious in terms of earning salvation. The Christian lives a morally good life not so that God will be indebted to him. Rather the Christian lives a good life because he is indebted to God. The Christian is not working his way up to God; rather God has come down to him.[43]

The problem with adopting either a pragmatic or moralistic approach is that they are unbiblical. They ultimately may produce the moral relativism that Christians want to avoid. Yet these two approaches are prevalent. The use of psychology and the use of marketing strategy are really just another way of viewing moralism and pragmatism. The tools of psychology can be employed by people of any faith and could lead adherents to shop around for a religion that meets their psychological needs better. The tools of marketing research are employed to produce results. They work, but since tough issues are avoided, morality could become relative under that type of preaching. What is needed is an approach to preaching that avoids these pitfalls, yet communicates the truths of Scripture without hedging or shading to a postmodern audience.

It is appropriate to discuss a manner of preaching that employs both the mandate for biblical proclamation and the necessity for communicating that message to postmoderns in a way that transforms lives. Expository preaching is the best model for remaining true to Scripture while connecting the transforming message of Scripture to a postmodern people.

v) **Expository preaching**

We have already looked closely at expository preaching as a model of communicating biblical truth. In that examination some comparative analysis relative to other models was developed. We have stated that broadly speaking, preaching can be categorised under four classifications based on their homiletic structure. These are: the textual sermon, the topical sermon, the textual-topical sermon and the expository sermon.[44] A brief recapitulation of these categories may be helpful before going on to discuss deductive and inductive modes of communication and ultimately embedding the inductive mode of expository preaching (with narrative elements) as the proposed *modus operandi* of homiletic practitioners.

The textual sermon draws its main idea directly from the text, but the divisions of the sermon do not necessarily follow in the same order or with the same flow as the original text. The topical sermon draws its main idea and points from some topic that the preacher chooses to develop. Starting with the topic the preacher then searches the Scriptures to find a particular passage or a selection of passages that teach some message on that topic. The third type of sermon, the textual-topical sermon is really a hybrid of the first two. The sermon idea and main points are derived from both the text and the topic. Of these four, the expository sermon is the superior sermon form, especially in a postmodern world.

First, the expository sermon draws the main idea, main points and subdivisions directly from the text, thereby maintaining the original order of the Scripture passage. The strength of this approach is found in its concern for maintaining the author's original intent and the purpose which the Holy Spirit intended when the passage was inspired.

Second, expository preaching is the one method of the four listed above that most strongly supports and defends a conservative doctrine of the inspiration of Scripture in that the thoughts and words of the Scripture writers are understood as inspired by the Holy Spirit and "profitable"[45]

Third, it prevents some of the inherent weaknesses in the other three methods, such as imposing ideas on the text, ignoring important theological truths, or developing a structure that fits the preacher's predisposition but not necessarily the original author's predilection.

Expository preaching is essentially grounded in exegesis. There is a stark contrast between exegesis and eisegesis. Eisegesis (from the Greek εινσηγεισθαι meaning "to lead in") is the process of interpretation of an existing text in such a way as to introduce one's own ideas. This is best understood when contrasted with exegesis. Exegesis (from the Greek ενξηγεισθαι, "to lead out") involves an extensive and critical interpretation of an authoritative text, especially sacred texts or Scripture, such as of the Old and New Testaments of *The Bible, The Talmud, The Midrash, The Koran* etc.[46] An exegete is a practitioner of this art. The word exegesis can mean explanation, but as a technical term it means "to draw the meaning out of" a given text. Exegesis may be contrasted with eisegesis, which means to read one's own interpretation into a given text. In general, exegesis presumes an attempt to view the text objectively, while eisegesis implies more subjectivity. One may encounter the terms exegesis and hermeneutics used interchangeably: there remains, however, a distinction. An exegesis is the interpretation and understanding of a text on the basis of the text itself. A hermeneutic is a practical application of a certain method or theory of interpretation, often revolving around the contemporary relevance of the text in question.

Traditional exegesis requires the following: analysis of significant words in the text in regard to translation; examination of the general historical and cultural context, confirmation of the limits of the passage, and lastly, examination of the context within the text.[47]

The expository preacher is an exegete, but the postmodern reader is an *eisegete*. While exegesis attempts to determine the historical context within which a particular verse exists - the so-called "*sitz im leben*" or "life setting", eisegetes often neglect this aspect of biblical study.[48] Exactly what constitutes eisegesis remains a moot point. Nevertheless the expository preacher believes in the importance of determining authorial intention within the text.

Postmodernists are suspicious of truth claims, especially when they consider them to be the opinions of an individual. Expository preaching represents the best approach to solving the dilemma of communicating truth, primarily because the truths are not the preacher's own, but the truth claims of God. In other words expository preaching takes its starting point from a view that God has revealed truth in the Scriptures. The role of the preacher is to bring that revelation to his hearers.

While this is the intent it does not necessarily follow that all members of the congregation will accept the message as one that comes from God. But no other sermon type holds as much promise for accomplishing that feat and doing so in a way that listeners can readily see this goal throughout the preaching event. Before explaining this approach in greater detail one other attractive characteristic of expository preaching may be identified. Of all the preaching models presented this is perhaps the most versatile. Expository preaching can be adapted to a wide variety of literary genre. It is just as effective when used for preaching narrative texts as it is for parables, poetry, prophecy, history and epistles. It can also be adapted to a variety of homiletic formats such as deductive, inductive and a combination of both. Haddon W. Robinson defines expository preaching as, "the communication of a Biblical concept, derived from and transmitted through a historical, grammatical, and literary study of a passage in its context, which the Holy Spirit first applies to the personality and experience of the preacher, then through him to his hearers."[49]

Several ideas emerge from this definition that illuminate what is meant by expository preaching. Clearly, as already established, it is preaching that depends upon a passage of Scripture as the foundation for the entire sermon. It may be spelled out again that this effectively means that rather than beginning with a topic or some idea from the mind of the preacher, the sermon flows entirely from the text. It is also preaching that communicates a concept that is derived from and transmitted through the passage in its context. The preacher who studies a text to determine the historical, grammatical and literary style must do more than preach the exegetical material. That material must be contextualised. Individual words and grammatical constructions are enlightening, but when separated from their context, they are possibly meaningless and potentially harmful.

Robinson points out that, orthodox theologians believe God has inspired, not just the thoughts of the original writer, but also the individual words.[50] These words must not be divorced from their original context, lest the preacher be guilty of substituting his own ideas in place of the inspired truths of Scripture.

Two other ideas emerge from Robinson's definition. He suggests that expository preaching occurs when the concept derived from the text is applied first to the expositor and then from the expositor to the hearers. This means that the truth must first be applied to the heart and personality of the preacher and then the hearers. When preachers stand up to deliver a sermon they are not just delivering a message from God, they are also delivering themselves. Robinson writes, "The audience does not hear the sermon, they hear the man."[51]

It was mentioned earlier that John Stott suggests that the task facing every preacher is bridging the chasm between the two horizons of the biblical text and the contemporary world.[52] He writes, "It is across this broad and deep divide of two thousand years of changing culture (more still in the case of the Old Testament) that Christian communicators have to throw bridges."[53] These two horizons mark a major distinctive in the expository approach. In expository preaching the sermon takes into consideration both the biblical world and the contemporary audience. Neither is diminished or excluded and in expository preaching the biblical text is the starting point for the sermon.[54] What is distinctive about these two elements is both the starting point, and the fact that both are included in the preparation and delivery process. This contrasts with topical preaching, which often begins with the audience in mind rather than the biblical text, and may in fact put more emphasis on the audience than on the biblical text.

John Piper has studied the preaching life of John Calvin and concluded that his commitment to expository preaching rested on three firm convictions. First, "Calvin believed that the Word had been taken away from the churches" and needed to be restored to the people.[55] Second, Calvin feared those who would preach from the pulpit their own ideas. He believed that, "by expounding Scripture as a whole, he would be forced to deal with all that God wanted to say, not just what he might want to say."[56] Third, Calvin saw majesty in the Word of God that manifested the majesty of God and he wanted that expressed through all of Geneva and the whole world in the context of his ministry and pastoral care.

Expository preaching, when properly utilised, carries both the authority of the Word of God and eliminates the trap of allowing the preacher's own imagination or pet ideas dominate the sermon in contradiction to God. In defence of expository preaching D. A. Carson offers six reasons why expository preaching should not be abandoned:

> (1) It is the method least likely to stray from Scripture, (2) It teaches people how to read their Bibles, (3) It gives confidence to the preacher and authorizes the sermon, (4) It meets the need for relevance without letting the clamor for relevance dictate the message, (5) It forces the preacher to handle the tough questions, and (6) It enables the preacher to expound systematically the whole counsel of God.[57]

One of the great benefits often mentioned by expositors is the way expository preaching can lend new colour and excitement to what may otherwise become rather dull. "Each new passage of Scripture adds fresh new insight to the 'old, old story' allowing it to live and breathe again with new life and vitality."[58] Martyn Lloyd-Jones provides clarification:

> True expository preaching is, therefore, doctrinal preaching, it is preaching which addresses specific truths from God to man. The expository preacher is not one who 'shares his studies' with others, he is an ambassador and a messenger, authoritatively delivering the Word of God to men. Such preaching presents a text, then with that text in sight throughout, there is deduction, argument and appeal, the whole making up a message which bears the authority of Scripture itself.[59]

Richard Mayhue provides a helpful summary, suggesting the following are minimal elements that identify expository preaching:
(1) The message finds its sole source in Scripture. (2) The message is extracted from Scripture through careful exegesis. (3) The message

preparation correctly interprets Scripture in its normal sense and its context. (4) The message clearly explains the original God-intended meaning of Scripture. (5) The message applies the Scriptural meaning for today.[60]

vi) Objections to expository preaching

Expository preaching has come under attack in recent years, especially in the light of postmodernism. David Hilborn's analysis of expository preaching lists four criticisms.[61] First, he says that expository preaching is "rationalistic", that it is a purely cerebral discipline that harkens back to Enlightenment modernity and fails to meet the emotive needs of postmoderns. Second, he argues that expository preaching is "elitist", that it leaves out at least 95% of the world's population because it requires a concentration span and linear logic that few possess. Third, he claims that it is "authoritarian", that postmoderns who have an aversion to authority will not respond to a didactic monologue that smacks of an assertion of power. And fourth, he argues that expository preaching is unbiblical, suggesting that expository preaching is not even employed by the human authors of Scripture or the characters in their narratives.[62]

If, by his use of the term "rationalistic", Hilborn is suggesting that expository preachers communicate through reason or logic, then his criticism is well founded, but it has been argued that expository preaching is firmly embedded in the revelation of Scripture. The biblical authors have communicated what they have heard, what they have seen with their eyes, and touched with their hands.[63] In other words, the Bible communicates objectively and expository preaching seeks to explain what the authors have communicated to their audience which includes the contemporary audience.

Hilborn's claim that expository preaching is elitist sounds suspiciously like the attitude of some educators who have systematically dumbed down curricula to meet the growing crisis in education. The church has always considered education an important part of ministry. To abandon exposition merely because it requires a sharper mind to understand complex theological truth can be compared to the practice during the middle ages of locking up the Scriptures behind bars and keeping the Bible out of the hands of the common people.[64]

The same argument holds for Hilborn's claim that that expository preaching is authoritarian. If by that the preacher is to avoid saying, "thus says the Lord" then preaching will be reduced to the opinions of an individual, rather than the revelation of God. If by authoritarian, Hilborn is suggesting that preachers should avoid dogmatism then he is correct. Expository preaching is authoritative but not authoritarian.

With regard to Hilborn's claim that expository preaching is unbiblical, an examination the Bible reveals that there is ample evidence that expository preaching, at least as defined above, is practiced throughout the Scriptures.

In Deuteronomy 4 Moses preaches an expository sermon on "a call to obedience". He cites the law given by God, and explains what God has said using examples, illustrations and applications. Anyone who reads the five books of Moses can readily see that Moses is an exemplar of expository preaching. This does not suggest that he avoids narrative. Clearly the book of Genesis and the Exodus experience are replete with narratives, but even these narratives serve to expound the nature of God and God's plan for the nation of Israel.

Assuming that the "Word of the Lord" represents the starting point for prophetic messages of the Old Testament, it could be argued that the major and minor prophets contain examples of expository preaching. Isaiah 53 is an expository sermon on the substitutionary atonement of the "Suffering Servant", who is recognised by New Testament scholars as Christ. Jonah proclaimed an expository sermon to Nineveh, "Yet forty days and Nineveh shall be overthrown!" (Jonah 3:4). Joel proclaimed the Word of the Lord and presented an expository sermon on the eschatological judgement of God (Joel 2:1-32). Hosea proclaimed an expository message on God's loyal covenant love, with a summons to repentance and promise of restoration (Hosea 14:1-9). Other examples abound. Accepting the premise that God's Word to the prophets is a beginning point for the sermon represents a parallel to beginning the sermon with the scriptural text.[65]

In the New Testament, while a great deal of material is narrative in nature, it is also filled with examples of exposition. For example, in Matthew 5—7, Jesus preaches the Sermon on the Mount and clearly utilises the tools of exposition. His practice there was to take the Old Testament law or teaching and explain it, illustrate it and apply it to the lives of his hearers. The epistles are also replete with exposition. The book of Hebrews is a masterful example of what is probably intended as a complete expository sermon. The writer of Hebrews quotes Old Testament passages, explains them, illustrates them and applies them to his contemporary audience.

One of the important elements of expository preaching that is often overlooked is its attention to literary genre. If the criticism of expository preaching suggests that all expository sermons are didactic, propositional lectures that ignore the narrative, parable, apocalyptic or poetic form of the passage, then that criticism is really against poorly conceived, poorly constructed and poorly communicated expository sermons. Expository preaching by its very definition utilises the literary genre and finds its structure in the passage that is being examined. To suggest that expository preaching violates the literary genre, by turning poetry into lecture is to do violence to the meaning of expository preaching as well as to Scripture itself.

The various literary genres of Scripture each exhibit certain characteristics that communicate truth in a variety of ways to different kinds of audiences. In fact, narrative, poetic and parabolic material has built-in elements which evoke emotion and invite the reader to enter into an experience with the text. Jesus used this technique often when he told parables. The audience hears that story and relates to the intended message. There are elements of both the subjective and objective in the parable. It is the subjective element, however, that causes the reader/hearer to understand the message Jesus was communicating.

Narrative material has the same effect. The Exodus narrative causes the reader to experience the tragedy and triumph of that oppressed nation. They learn that God knows what they are going through and God cares. The twenty-third Psalm is a wonderful piece of poetry that evokes emotion and puts the reader in touch with a subjective response to God.

Preaching the epistles requires that the expositor explore the context of the letter to determine the specific need being addressed or the circumstances that led to the writing of the letter. Sometimes this means that passages are understood as culturally conditioned.

Expository preaching can meet the challenge of helping those who need subjective elements before they accept an objective proposition. The expository method handles this objection more faithfully and successfully than any other method. There is some merit in the postmodernist's definition of socially constructed truth which must be taken into consideration in explaining a text of Scripture. To do so with sensitivity and compassion is part of what it means to be a preacher. Christianity remains a *dominant* worldview but it need not be exercised as power in a *domineering* way.

Expository preaching can be utilised effectively by preaching expository sermons with some modifications. Haddon Robinson acknowledged this in an interview, "expository preaching is primarily a matter of sermon philosophy rather than sermon form. Expositors are not restricted to a homiletical strait jacket that is purely deductive."[66]

vii) The essence and extremes of expository preaching

There is a great deal of work going on within theology which upholds the value of preaching, especially expository preaching. This work has been unequivocal in asserting that this kind of preaching provides the best model for attaining God's intended purposes through the preaching act. There is, however, disagreement and debate about the meaning of "expository preaching".[67] Its meaning is nevertheless generally understood as a style of preaching which derives its content from the biblical text and accurately expounds what the text means. This is the essence of expository preaching, and its essential elements are directed toward informing, influencing and altering attitudes and actions, or accomplishing whatever the passage of Scripture intends. Sidney Greidanus, speaking on this issue says of the Bible, "...it is the *only* normative course for contemporary preaching...because it alone provides the normative *proclamation* of God's redemption and the response he requires. The Bible itself, therefore, can be seen as preaching."[68]

The nineteenth century preacher and contemporary of C. H. Spurgeon, Joseph Parker, wrote these inspirational and insightful words about what a preacher should be:

> ...a man to tell us the meaning of hard words and difficult things and mysteries which press too heavily upon our staggering faith. The interpretation comes to us as a lamp, we instantly feel the comfort and the liberty of illumination...men who can turn foreign words, difficult languages, into our mother tongue...and that which was difficulty before becomes a gate opening upon a wide liberty. We need a man who can interpret to us the meaning of confused and confusing...events; some man with a key from heaven, some man with divine insight, the vision that sees the poetry and the reality of things...[69]

This statement of what is required of the preacher needs to be balanced, however, by avoiding the legacy of medieval scholasticism. The thrust in preaching ought to lead to the *application* of truth and not merely the *understanding* of truth. Words can be described in context and the grammatical relation to the sentence explained, truth can be dissected, inspected and digested but that does not constitute preaching. This kind of scholasticism is a cognitive activity marked by "sophisticated dialectal method".[70] Dargan states the nature of the problem of medieval scholasticism, "The metaphysical subtleties, hair-splitting distinctions, attenuated reasonings, the dogmas, fancies, speculations about things of no particular consequence then or now, all became in some measure the possession of the pulpit."[71] This is not to deny the value of scholarship *per se*, as it has contributed enormously to biblical studies. The influence of scholasticism in style of preaching has; however, had a lasting and damaging effect.[72]

viii) Preaching that connects with postmoderns

Research in communication theory and the cultural analysis of Leonard Sweet has provided some insight into approaches that connect with postmoderns. Since the 1960's researchers have studied the effect of communication on both sides of the brain and concluded that the left side of the brain is more linear and the right side more non-verbal, spatial, emotional and image dependent.[73] This knowledge of the two sides of the brain has suggested that preaching take into account both sides of the brain. Jim Somerville suggests that preaching should be directed to both sides of the brain. He says preaching to the right brain should use vivid language, metaphors, and images. Preachers should help listeners move from one way of thinking to another, explore the unusual, and leave some things open-ended.[74] In addition to brain research, it was noted earlier that Leonard Sweet's cultural analysis has suggested that preaching include elements that are "experiential, participatory and image laden and connective."[75]

It has been argued that expository preaching is the best method of preaching for ensuring faithfulness to the Word of God. It has also been noted that postmodernism presents challenges to preaching. Taking into consideration the areas of weakness already noted in the deductive model, it is time to examine an approach that takes into consideration the challenge of postmodernism, research into communications, and Sweet's cultural analysis.

ix) The inductive approach

There are basically two approaches for presenting ideas, whether in a sermon or in any other type of discourse: the deductive approach and the inductive approach.[76] The deductive approach begins by stating a proposition or truth and then proceeds to explain, illustrate and apply that truth. This approach is rather traditional and probably one of the easiest ways to preach a sermon or teach a lesson. From a postmodern perspective, there are difficulties with this approach. Postmodern listeners may feel that the preacher is assuming too much authority or worse;

articulating his own opinions. They may respond: "that may be your truth but I don't agree."

If the listener rejects the stated proposition, the sermon may fail before the preacher ever gets started. One could argue that preaching then becomes apologetic; that is to say, stating the proposition and then setting out to prove it. Again, from a postmodern perspective, this may fail if the postmodern listener rejects the logic of the arguments or simply believes that truth is so relative that they reject the proposition no matter what evidence is presented.

The alternative is the inductive approach. The inductive approach, rather than beginning with a stated proposition, begins where the hearers are and works toward the proposition which may or may not be stated at the end of the sermon. Haddon Robinson noted that good expository preaching can be arranged, "deductively, semi-inductively or inductively."[77]

Fred Craddock suggests that civilisation has changed over the years from a predominantly oral society to a literal society and now to an aural society.[78] He explains that culture once learned primarily by sharing oral traditions that were passed down from person to person. Then with the advent of the printing press, people began to learn through reading the printed text. Today, with television and radio, culture now hears a message that is mediated by mechanical devices, and they are free to tune in or tune out.[79] This pattern of socialising has made society more impersonal. Gone are the days when families sat around in a circle and listened to the stories of the elders. Now they sit together in front of a television screen or they sit alone in front of the television or computer screen. Sitting in a church with a group of people that may be strangers to them and listening to a minister with whom they may feel disconnected, telling them things they ought to believe, seems strange. The deductive pattern of preaching with its stated proposition, front-loading the message, invites the audience to tune out, not only because they reject the proposition, but also because that is not the way they receive information.

It may be helpful to think of it this way: no one tells a joke by first stating the punch line and then going on to explain the details. Similarly nobody tells the moral of a story and then sets out to tell the story. Whether one agrees with the moral or not, nobody wants to hear the story that way. Postmodern listeners have grown up on movies and television shows that invite the viewers to experience the story by building drama and excitement up to the very end, leaving the audience with a sense that they have experienced the story themselves. Most people are engaged by a mystery which needs to be solved. Television producers and film directors build the drama of a story in such a way that the audience tries to solve the mystery and guess at the conclusion all along the way. If the writers told the end of the story at the beginning, some viewers might watch, but most would tune out. Fred Craddock offers this cogent illustration contrasting the two approaches:

> Watch an old man peel an apple for his grandson. Forget the sanitation problems and watch the deliberate care in beginning, the slow curl of unbroken peel, the methodical removing of the core. The boy's eyes enlarge, his saliva flows, he urges more speed, he is at the point of pouncing upon grandfather and seizing the apple. Then it is given to him, and it is the best apple in the world. Place beside that small drama a sermon that gives its conclusion, breaks it into points and applications and one senses the immensity of the preacher's crime against the normal currents of life.[80]

Ralph and Greg Lewis suggest that the key to inductive preaching is, "getting listeners involved in the sermon."[81] They point out that preachers have experienced that shift in the congregation when a story is told. Spurgeon said illustrations are the windows that let light into our sermons.[82] This truth has tempted many a preacher to preach what Chuck Swindoll called "skyscraper sermons", one story on top of another. No doubt that approach may be appealing to some audiences, but it may leave them with a rather weak diet.

The approach Ralph and Gregg Lewis advocate is an inductive approach that involves the audience in much the same way that illustrations involve the listeners. "An inductive sermon is one that starts where the people are, with particular elements—the narrative, dialogue, analogy, questions, parables, the concrete experiences—and then leads to general conclusions."[83] Rather than stating the conclusions at the beginning, the preacher builds the excitement of the truth he is teaching, involving the listeners in the process until both arrive at the conclusion together.

This approach meets a critical need in postmoderns. They tend to reject authority and absolutes, fearing that the opinions of others may be biased by power structures. Inductive preaching allows them to arrive at the truth without feeling that some proposition has been imposed on them from an authority figure.

This does not mean that the preacher must abdicate authority, as many feel Craddock has advocated in his inductive approach.[84] The preacher who uses this approach, rather than stating a truth he must defend or prove, demonstrates the defence and proof of his thesis throughout the sermon so that the listeners arrive at his central thesis as if it were their own. As Ralph and Gregg Lewis point out, "a sermon can be factually correct, homiletically sound, biblically accurate, doctrinally orthodox and still achieve nothing because it fails to involve the listeners."[85] Involvement is the key. And listener involvement is the strength of the inductive process in preaching.

x) Contrasting the deductive and inductive approaches

Expository preaching can be done in an inductive fashion which preserves all of its strengths while avoiding some of its weaknesses. In the light of the challenge presented by postmodernism, an inductive approach to expository preaching offers the greatest promise for meeting the challenge and reaching postmoderns in the pews.

Ralph and Gregg Lewis have presented some insightful contrasts between the deductive and inductive process that represents a clear indication that the inductive approach is a superior method of sermon construction and delivery, especially in the context of the paradigm shift.[86] In deductive sermons, the preacher begins with generalisations, assertions and propositions. In inductive sermons, the preacher begins with the particulars that lead to the conclusions or propositions and delays the assertions until the hearers have come to the same conclusions.[87] For the postmodern listener, this allows time for processing the truth and sensing that they are involved in the process. In the deductive sermon, the preacher begins where the speaker is, not necessarily where the listener is; while in the inductive sermon, the preacher begins where the listener is.[88] This means that the preacher will have to determine the contemporary need that the text addresses. It does not suggest that the preacher discovers a need and then searches Scripture for a solution. That can lead to proof-texting. In deductive preaching, there may be an air of personal prejudice, while in the inductive sermon the preacher allows the facts and particulars of life to speak.[89]

Postmoderns reject the Christian metanarrative. But the inductive approach offers postmodern listeners opportunity to enter into the biblical narrative and claim it as their own.[90] What before may have seemed like an incursive narrative may become for them part of their own story. This is certainly part of what it means to be a Christian: the biblical story of paradise lost and paradise regained becomes personal.

Sometimes the deductive approach gives unwanted and unwarranted advice before any common ground is established, but in the inductive approach, the preacher saves the advice until the listener has arrived at the same conclusions the preacher actually held from the beginning.[91] Since postmoderns believe that truth is subjective, they are more apt to go on a journey in discovery of truth than they are to accept that the preacher's truth is automatically their truth. The inductive approach does not abdicate authority. It helps to uphold the authority of Scripture by allowing the Bible to speak for itself. Conservatives have had a tendency to go to great lengths to prove that Scripture is inerrant or authoritative. In fact, this defensive posture has sometimes sent the wrong message; that it is so weak it needs help.

The deductive approach comes off as authoritarian and sometimes assumes an adversarial posture; while the inductive approach achieves authority and proceeds in a non-adversarial manner.[92] Inductive preaching shares the experience and the process so that the listener is not in a sparring match with the preacher who must prove his point. This does not suggest that inductive preaching is not persuasive preaching. Quite the contrary, an inductive sermon can be very persuasive. If the fruits of exegesis produce evidence to support the central claim, then let that evidence be presented first so that the conclusion becomes as obvious to listeners as it is to preachers.

Deductive preaching is often rational rather than relational; while the inductive approach is more relational than rational.[93] Postmoderns who have rejected modernistic rationalism will appreciate a relational approach that is more holistic and takes into consideration the heart as well as the head. The deductive approach can be irrelevant, show a lack of respect for hearers, and subject-centred rather than person-centred. The inductive approach, on the other hand, relates to real life and human experiences, it respects the opinions of the hearers, and focuses on the human needs of the hearers at a personal level.[94]

Some might argue that the approach is not biblical. Ralph and Gregg Lewis point out that God's method of communication is more in line with the inductive approach than the deductive approach. They write that God:

>...doesn't start his *Bible* message by saying, 'I'm going to prove my loving faithfulness by presenting the world with a means of salvation from sin and death'. Instead, God begins by recounting his specific acts in history and tries to sustain their intensity in ever-increasing scope.[95]

Careful reading of Scripture would sustain this argument. God's revelation is progressive. Consider the approach used in many of the New Testament books. In both the gospel of John and the first epistle of John, the apostle refrains from overtly stating his theme until the very end. The theme of the Gospel of John is found in, "Now Jesus did many other signs in the presence of the disciples, which are not written in this book; but these are written so that you may believe that Jesus is the Christ, the Son of God, and that by believing you may have life in his name." (John 20:30-31). And in 1 John, the apostle withholds his theme until 1 John 5:13, "I write these things to you who believe in the name of the Son of God that you may know that you have eternal life." It is certainly helpful to turn to the end of these books to find the theme before preaching them, but John didn't write his books that way.

xi) Integrating both expository sermon and inductive approach

Haddon Robinson has included in his book, *Expository Preaching*, a section on the inductive arrangement. He wrote "Inductive sermons produce a sense of discovery in listeners, as though they arrived at the idea on their own. Induction is particularly effective with indifferent or hostile audiences likely to reject a preacher's proposition were it presented early in the sermon."[96] If any audience is likely to be "indifferent or hostile" it is the postmodern in the pew. John A. Broadus, in his book entitled, *On the Preparation and Delivery of Sermons*, includes the inductive argument as a key form of sermon development. He wrote that, "Induction is, in popular usage, the most common form of argument."[97] In fact, Robinson suggests sixteen sermon patterns and all but one of them are inductive arrangements.[98]

xii) Narrative preaching

David Larsen notes that Hans Frei, in, *The Eclipse of Biblical Narrative* pointed out the inherent danger of treating all literary genres in exactly the same way. He argued that, "instead of fitting ourselves into the biblical world as represented in Scripture and feeling the excitement and force of a narrative, we have tended to neuter the text in a vain effort to fit the biblical world into our own agenda."[99] Narrative preaching opens up a whole new avenue for reaching postmoderns. In keeping with the suggestions Leonard Sweet has made that preaching incorporates experiential, participatory, image-laden and connective elements, a narrative style can accomplish this.

The stories of the Bible invite the listener to experience the tragedies and triumphs of biblical characters. A good narrative sermon will bring the audience into the story and allow them to relate to the experiences of the ancient world. Narrative sermons are inherently participatory. The listeners are working toward solving the mystery or sensing the climactic moment along with the preacher. The narratives of Scripture are already image-laden and may need only minor explanation to bring them into contemporary understanding.

Finally, narratives are great vehicles for helping the contemporary audience connect with the biblical characters and recognise that they too can connect with God. Obviously a good sermon should move the listeners to make some response to the message. If postmoderns need to connect, as Sweet has argued, then preaching should give them an opportunity to connect with Jesus.

Lowry has developed a pattern for sermon development which he calls "the homiletical plot".[100] The idea of forming the sermon as a plot means that the preacher develops the sermon so that a tension exists which calls for some resolution. In order to frame the sermon as a homiletic plot, Lowry suggests finding the "itch" and then helping the audience discover how to "scratch" the itch.[101]

Lowry's pattern for development in *The Homiletical Plot* involves five stages. These are, (1) upsetting the equilibrium, (2) analysing the discrepancy, (3) disclosing the clue to resolution, (4) experiencing the gospel, and (5) anticipating the consequences.[102]

The first stage in the development, "upsetting the equilibrium" involves creating a sense of ambiguity. Lowry quotes Dewy as saying, "thinking begins at the point of a felt problem."[103] This is the itch. The ambiguity involved in a problem causes the audience to begin thinking about solutions or feeling the urgency of the problem.

The second stage, "analysing the discrepancy", is a diagnostic phase. In this stage, the preacher probes the problem with questions of "why?" The preacher may say, "is this the problem? Is it this? Is it that?" The goal is to allow the tension to continue to build.

The third stage, "disclosing the clue to resolution" has a key element. It includes a "reversal" which brings a surprise.[104] This is the plot twist that catches the audience by surprise and often makes the difference in overcoming hostility or unbelief, "Once the clue to resolution is articulated, the hearer is ready to receive the Word—to discover how the gospel of Jesus Christ intersects the human predicament."[105]

Lowry's fourth stage, "experiencing the gospel" develops more fully this clue to resolution. If the stage has been set, then the gospel message is ripe for telling. For the postmodern listener, this process will help them "abduct" the truth. The message of the gospel can become; not some alien metanarrative, but their own story. They see themselves in the sermon and recognise the tension that has been building and are surprised to discover that this message is directed at them.

Lowry's fifth stage, "anticipating the consequences" moves the sermon toward an appeal for a response. He suggests that there are three approaches to relieving the tension created in the sermon and moving the person toward decision. To "push" the person from behind and magnify the consequences; this can reduce the tension and "pull" the person toward decision by revealing the possibilities; or use a combination of the two approaches.[106] Most people are turned off by guilt trips and a heavy push that emphasises the negative consequences may push a person toward more hostility and less openness.

Lowry admits that, "the term consequences, does carry some unnecessary freight."[107] In a more recent formulation of the homiletic plot he proposes that in order to overcome this obstacle and provide a simpler format, there are just four stages in the reformulation: *conflict, complication, sudden shift* and *unfolding*.[108] The first two stages are virtually the same, just renamed; however, the third and fourth stages, "disclosing the clue to resolution" and "experiencing the gospel" are subsumed under the single term, "sudden shift". "Unfolding" includes some carry over from "experiencing the gospel" and "anticipating the consequences". McLaren suggests that a story abducts one's attention and sustains that attention until the hearer has done some thinking.

Jay Adams proposes a plot development that may even be simpler than Lowry's. He suggests five stages should be labelled: (1) background, (2) a complication or problem, (3) suspense, (4) climax, and (5) conclusion.[109] Buttrick is another advocate of plot and instead of using the term "points" in a sermon, he suggests the term, "moves".[110] This may be the best way to write the sermon outline, by noting the various moves and the elements that should be included under each movement in the sermon.

xiii) The essentials of a good sermon for postmoderns

Jay Adams suggests that there are five essentials of a good sermon. These are essentially the same for sermons directed toward postmoderns.

First, a good sermon for postmoderns is *preaching*. It is not a string of stories or a stodgy lecture; it is preaching that brings the Bible alive and enables people to hear from God.[111] There has been some debate in the last few centuries over whether there is a distinction between preaching and teaching. In the New Testament, the Greek words κηρύσσω (*kerússo*) and ευαγγελλίζω (*euaggellízo*) are normally translated "preaching" and διδάσκω (*didásko*), is normally translated "teaching". In some cases they are used together in the same sentence as if they are interchangeable.[112] However, there may be at least a subtle distinction between the two terms.

In biblical usage, "preaching" is more often related to the gospel and the kingdom of God; whereas, "teaching" covers a broader range of issues.[113] In our contemporary setting, teaching has taken on the meaning of an *informative* presentation; whereas preaching is often characterised as a more *transformative* presentation. It could be argued that the Scripture's use of both terms is aimed at transformation. Preaching should do more than merely inform. Postmoderns are typically suspicious of knowledge claims, but might welcome a transforming experience. A good sermon for postmoderns is preaching with a goal toward transformation.

Second, a good sermon for postmoderns is *biblical* preaching. It is not a lecture on some truth, philosophy, or the ideas of some public figure. It is a sermon that proclaims Scripture with authority. Expository preaching also preserves the sufficiency of Scripture. Steven J. Rawson demonstrates the "supernatural potency" of the Scripture when the expository method is employed. He points out that Scripture possesses the "power to connect", the "power to convict", the "power to convert", the "power to conform", the "power to counsel" and the "power to conquer".[114]

Third, a good sermon for postmoderns is *interesting*. The preacher draws every possible bit of substance out of the passage and presents it like a fine chef. Adams wrote, "Men and women (and especially young people) are being turned away from Christ and his church by dull, uninteresting, unedifying and aimless preaching."[115] Sermons should be interesting. An interesting sermon has a single focus. Haddon Robinson calls this the "big idea".[116] A sermon that teaches too many different ideas can quickly lose people. Paul Wilson has made a strong case for this single focus, suggesting that in order to prevent aimless wandering, preachers should, "be guided by six signs along the highway of sermon composition." He says preachers should identify: one text, one theme, one doctrine, one need, one image and one mission.[117]

An interesting sermon targets a specific felt need. This comes about by good exegesis of the congregation as well as the text. As pointed out earlier, the five unique needs of postmoderns that Amy Mears and Charles Bugg suggested provide a helpful starting point. They suggested the five needs that are often overlooked include, "the need for acceptance, the need for hope, the need for ecological awareness, the need for inclusion, and the need for distinctiveness."[118] It has also been noted that postmoderns have unique epistemological needs that can be met by understanding their aversion to metanarratives, the employment of a hermeneutic of suspicion and the use of deconstruction. Sermons that meet felt needs make a sermon more interesting.

Another ingredient in interesting sermons involves the style of delivery. An inductive approach captures greater interest and a narrative style keeps listeners involved in the sermon. The use of illustrations, images and metaphors are powerful tools for understanding and they have the added benefits of relaxing an audience and keeping them interested. Sermons which have a single focus, meet felt needs and include vivid illustrative material produce interesting sermons for postmoderns.

A good sermon for postmoderns is well organised. It moves with purpose and direction. The thought is clear. It has balance and meaning. Whether the passage is didactic, narrative, parable, apocalyptic, or poetic the sermon should have good organisation which compliments the type of literary genre, the purpose of the passage and the best approach to good communication. Sermons that wander around looking for a point will leave the audience bored and confused. Even sermons that proceed in narrative moves have a point, a focus, a purpose and an application. Keeping the congregation focused toward achieving the purpose of the sermon is probably the best defence against a poorly organised sermon.

A good sermon for postmoderns is practical. It not only tells what God has said, it tells how to do what God has commanded.[119] The goal in preaching to postmoderns is to bring about transformation. The Word of God is not constructed merely as a historical book about ancient people: it is a handbook for living. Application should reflect this practical dimension of the sermon. Clear, targeted applications demonstrate not only *what* must be done, but *how* it is done with God's help. In short, a good sermon is biblical proclamation that is interesting, well-organised and practical.

The veracity and value of preaching will not, however, be readily accepted by postmoderns who perceive it as an antiquated mode of communication which is essentially authoritarian. There is still a gap to be bridged and if this is to be done effectively a distinction needs to be made between preaching which is authoritative and preaching which is authoritarian. The former has some possibility of engaging postmoderns; the latter is problematic and more likely to alienate those seeking to encounter God.

xiv) Preaching that persuades

The notion of persuasion in postmodern culture has to be reconceived. It is not to be equated with the modernist notion where it is essentially about being intellectually convinced of the veracity of an argument. It should, rather, be understood in classical terms. Ancient Greek and Roman civilisation was devoted to the dynamics of public-speaking. Plato, Aristotle, Cicero and others contributed to the development of the rhetorical art form. Aristotle's seminal work, *Rhetoric*, was the standard text for the times. Aristotle had a particular genius for systematising knowledge and in this work he categorises the rhetorical art of persuasion in three divisions. Firstly, he deals with *ethos*, which focuses on the integrity of the speaker. Secondly, he deals with *logos*, which is about the inherent logic of the message itself. Thirdly, he deals with *pathos*, which is about the emotions evoked by the oration. Ian Pitt-Watson points to a contemporary failure to address the emotional nature of people:

> Unless there is some measure of emotional involvement on the part of the preacher and on the part of his hearers the *kerygma* cannot be heard in its fullness for the *kerygma* speaks to the whole man, emotions and all, and simply does not make sense to the intellect and the will alone.[120]

There are certain parallels between this Aristotelian contribution to rhetorical analysis and homiletic practice. The integrity of the preacher, the authority of the Word and the appeal to emotions are all relevant factors in preaching. In modernism the stress was on the authority of the Word (*logos*) above the others (*ethos* and *pathos*). But in postmodernism there is an emphasis on emotions, where truth is seen as a matter of individual belief and morality is governed by the principle, "if it feels good, it is good." Donald McCullough asserts:

> The vehemence of the debate over controversial issues—such as language about God, the inerrancy of Scripture, abortion, creation and evolution, the role of women in leadership, ordination of homosexuals, and others—too often breeds arrogant certainty. Instead of an enriching exchange leading to greater discernment, we have shouting matches that shut off dialogue and fragment the Christian community. One must ask: Who is being served in all this—God or the God of my understanding?[121]

The importance of the preacher's integrity cannot be underestimated. His moral character may influence how the message itself is perceived. Augustine said, "The life of the speaker has greater weight in determining whether he is obediently heard than any grandness of eloquence."[122]

Certainly a lack of integrity undermines credibility. There is a connection between preaching and practice insofar as the moral stature of the messenger contributes to enhancing receptivity to the message. Nevertheless, effectiveness in preaching is not ultimately determined by the eloquence of the preacher, the soundness of his logic, the virtue of the man or indeed all of these factors combined. George Whitfield's biographer comments:

> ...Whitfield's...effectiveness lay not in his eloquence or zeal. As we look back from our present standpoint we see that God's chosen time to 'arise and have mercy upon Zion...yea, the set time had come,' and that in raising up Whitfield, He had granted upon him and his ministry 'a mighty effusion of the Holy Ghost': and it was this, the Divine power, which was the first secret of his success.[123]

The Christian preacher would assert that there is a supernatural element in the event or process of conversion. Oswald Sanders speaks of the herald of the gospel in these terms, "...he prepares the way, clears the way and gets out of the way."[124] Nevertheless, the elements listed above, at worst, cannot hinder the communication process and probably enhance it. Robinson comments:

> In an earlier generation, it was enough for a preacher to announce the truth, and the congregation would ratify it. Today such pronouncements are met with resistance. Today, I have to persuade people, even in the church, of the gospel and its implications. I must respect the right of an audience to make up its own mind. Today's listeners can feel at a gut level the difference between persuading and pronouncing. They react to preaching that doesn't respect their freedom to make up their own minds.[125]

An examination of Paul's thinking and methods of communication provide insight into preaching in a postmodern context by showing that his success is never attributed to convincing people of the veracity of propositional truth claims. It was not enough for Paul to announce the truth, either evangelistically, as revealed in the book of Acts, or pastorally as revealed in his epistles. Paul's preaching met with resistance too. Paul had to persuade people then, even in the church, of the gospel and its implications (for example, Galatians). The key point in Robinson's comment (above) is to realise that there is a difference between "persuading" and "pronouncing". It is a difference in attitude and tone that is almost intuitively conveyed, but it is an important difference in a world where style takes precedence over substance. John MacArthur put it cogently, "True biblical preaching ought to be a life-changing endeavour. The conscientious preacher does not merely seek to impart abstract doctrine or plain facts to his people; he also pleads with them for heartfelt and earnest obedience."[126]

Paul's approach to presenting the gospel involved *reasoning, explaining* and *proving* in an effort to see people persuaded. He used his intellectual faculties and theological training to demonstrate the truth of his message by drawing on evidence from Old Testament Scripture. The Bereans tested the accuracy of his claims by searching the Scriptures in order to establish the validity of his assertions.[127] A number of them found that there was sufficient evidence to warrant a verdict of proven and yielded to its consequential demand for faith. [128]

Paul lived in that world where rhetoric was revered. He was deemed to be a failure as an orator by some. He alludes to this issue in his second letter to the Corinthian church.[129] Paul did not, however, merely employ the oratorical skill of the sophist in seeking to convey the gospel. Conscious of his limitations he asserts that it was the power of God that penetrated the hearts of the Corinthians.[130]

Nevertheless, Paul did seek to persuade people of the truth of the gospel. This is clear in Acts chapters 17-19 in particular. It is revealed that in Thessalonica, "as was his custom, and on three Sabbath days he *reasoned* with them from the Scriptures, *explaining* and *proving* that it was necessary for the Christ to suffer and to rise from the dead...(vs. 2-3, emphasis added by italicization).

Clearly Paul is engaged in expository preaching of the Old Testament in a reasonable, rational and persuasive manner. Then Paul travels to Athens and there, "he *reasoned* in the synagogue with the Jews and the devout persons, and in the marketplace every day with those who happened to be there" (v.17, emphasis added by italicization). Paul stood up at the meeting in the Areopagus and said, "Men of Athens, I perceive that in every way you are very religious. For as I passed along and observed the objects of your worship, I found also an altar with this inscription, 'To the unknown god'. What therefore you worship as unknown, this I proclaim to you." (vs. 22-23).

This is a masterstroke of rhetoric in the service of the gospel. When in Corinth Paul continued with the same approach, "And he *reasoned* in the synagogue every Sabbath, and tried to *persuade* Jews and Greeks" (Acts 18:4, emphasis added by italicization). This chapter also highlights the fact that Paul's enemies knew him to be a person who sought to persuade others to convert from Judaism to Christianity, "But when Gallio was proconsul of Achaia, the Jews made a united attack on Paul and brought him before the tribunal, saying, 'This man is *persuading* people to worship God contrary to the law'" (Acts 18:12-13, emphasis added by italicization).

In Ephesus Paul is found arguing persuasively, "And he entered the synagogue and for three months spoke boldly, *reasoning* and *persuading* them about the kingdom of God" (19:8, emphasis added by italicization).

He stayed in Ephesus for two years and had daily discussions in the lecture hall of Tyrannus. When Festus accused Paul of insanity Paul replied that what he was saying was true and reasonable, "I am not out of my mind, most excellent Festus, but I am speaking true and rational words." (Acts 26:25). Dabney exhorts preachers:

> Let your aim be to persuade men in Christ's name, and not to be praised for skill in persuading...You must so hunger for the salvation of the souls before you, that you shall desire to make the effect of sacred truth fill them...He is not the true preacher who sends his hearers home exclaiming, 'How eloquent the minister today; how beautiful his imagery; how artful his arrangement; how skilful his argument and persuasion!'[131]

This stresses the spiritual dimension to the activity of preaching. The great evangelistic apostle was very conscious that it was not enticing words or eloquence that prevailed upon people to be receptive and responsive to the message. He does not attribute their conversions to plausible argumentation. He attributes the "success" of his preaching to the operation of the power of the Holy Spirit in stirring the minds and emotions of his hearers to persuade them to yield their wills to the will of God. Calvin said there is no benefit from preaching, "except when God shines in us by the light of his Spirit..."[132] Spurgeon referred to this work of the Spirit in preaching as, "the sacred anointing."[133] Paul never set out to impress the Corinthians with semantics. He believed in the idea expressed by the writer to the Hebrews, "For the word of God is living and active, sharper than any two-edged sword, piercing to the division of soul and of spirit, of joints and of marrow, and discerning the thoughts and intentions of the heart" (4:12). Tony Sargent describes the sacred unction of the Spirit in these terms:

> ...the penetration and dominion of the personality by the Spirit...It is the preacher gliding on eagle's wings, soaring high, swooping low, carrying and being carried along by a dynamic other than his own. His consciousness of what is happening is not obliterated. He is not in a trance. He is being worked on but is aware that he is still working. He is being spoken through but he knows he is still speaking. The words are his but the facility with which they come compels him to realise that the source is beyond himself.[134]

Paul preached Christ with passion and power and sought to be as persuasive as possible in the manner in which he presented his message. His discourse was rational and coherent and characterised by a fervent desire to see people coming to faith in Christ. It is obvious that others recognised this tone in his preaching. This is evident in the following words, "And Agrippa said to Paul, 'In a short time would you *persuade* me to be a Christian?'" (Acts 26:28, emphasis added by italicisation). In his second letter to the Corinthians Paul explicitly states that he intentionally set about seeking to persuade people of the truth of the gospel, "Therefore, knowing the fear of the Lord, we *persuade* others." (5:11, emphasis added by italicisation).

Ajith Fernando points out that, "The word *peitho* (persuade) is used at least eight times in Acts to refers to the evangelism of the early Christians."[135] Fernando goes on to point out that "when persuasion is used in connection with religious proclamation today it is often associated with arrogance and intolerance."[136] Fernando draws attention to how peculiar this is:

> This is strange because persuasion is used daily in many spheres of life. Advertisers seek to persuade us to patronize certain products, and politicians seek to persuade us to accept their policies and vote for them. Yet when it comes to religion, this approach to communication is considered inappropriate.[137]

He then identifies inappropriate kinds of persuasion such as "imposition" and "manipulation."[138]

Paul was aware that the truth of the gospel is not discovered through deductive or inductive reasoning alone. He argued that fathoming the things of God is a matter of spiritual discernment. It is the Holy Spirit that enables the mind to apprehend truth and that intellectual comprehension stimulates impulses that determine decisions. In the words of Calvin, "The effectual cause of faith is not the perspicacity of our mind, but the calling of God."[139] In this sense then, it is not what is *discovered* by the human mind but what is *disclosed* by the divine mind. It is not, therefore, merely a mental matter. Paul was aware that coming to know divine truth was not the result of *speculation* but rather the result of *revelation* and *illumination*. He clearly communicated this to the Corinthians when he said, "The natural person does not accept the things of the Spirit of God, for they are folly to him, and he is not able to understand them because they are spiritually discerned." (1 Corinthians 2:14).

Nevertheless, he did what he could to make the message clear and intelligible. Again the book of Acts confirms this. Whether it was the synagogue or the marketplace, Paul laboured day after day to present the gospel in as persuasive a manner as possible. This was also his typical approach in Thessalonica[140] and Ephesus.[141]

There is evidence in Acts 17 of some degree of interaction with his listeners: his style had some discursive features. He was essentially handling an abstract idea in a pedagogical manner, but something of his passionate concern for his listeners must have been evident. Christ also taught pedagogically (Sermon on the Mount) but he was frequently questioned by either people who were looking for answers or looking to trip him up. So Jesus had to deal not only with supportive questions but also with hostile ones.

In the postmodern climate the rules of engagement have changed. Argumentation in Paul's day was based on the refined outcome of centuries of Greek thought. There was an established framework for determining truth claims. Rules of logic may not be perfect but to discard them altogether is absurd. D. A. Carson speaks of this revolt against absolutes:

> For the first time in the history of the church…the only heresy that's left is the view that there is such a thing as heresy—that is the one heretical view. And within this kind of framework to preach an unflinching truth, and to claim that apart from this truth men and women are eternally lost makes you not only sound 'nineteenth century' and bigoted, but irrelevant and hopelessly lost in an epistemology now dead just crying out for a decent burial.[142]

According to Scripture, God reasons with sinners.[143] But God is not negotiating terms and conditions or conferring with man in order to reach a mutually satisfactory agreement. Nevertheless this text indicates that the revelation of the biblical God is of one who invites people to consider their condition in propositional terms that promises the prospect of forgiveness.

If Paul is taken to be a superior model of effective communication to which Christian preachers should aspire, then his style must be scrutinised to see what principles may be extrapolated from such a model. It is instructive to note, therefore, how frequently he uses the phrase "I beseech you". He is unashamed to implore, entreat and earnestly beg believers to become what God wants them to be. If this tone of urging and exhorting is absent from preaching it becomes less than what it ought to be. John MacArthur says:

> After all, to be hearers of the Word without being doers is to be dangerously deceived (James 1:22). And one sure way for preachers to cultivate hearers-only is to deliver nothing more than dry, didactic lectures—dull performances for the intellectually curious. That is not biblical preaching, no matter how sound the teaching may be on an academic level.[144]

Passion is an important element of preaching. If preaching is merely didactic and pedantic in seeking to convey information to the mind alone then people may understand the meaning of the message but fall short of undertaking its demands. Certainly, preaching is an exercise that has a pedagogical dimension but if a sermon is presented like a lecture or a dissertation on a theme, in a manner that is cold-blooded, detached and distant it may convince the intellect but not captivate the soul. Preaching to the soul not only engages the mind, emotions and will but also addresses the desires and moral inclinations of people.

On the other hand a highly charged and histrionic harangue, however earnest it may be, might electrify the emotions without engaging the mind. Truth must be spoken to the mind with calculated intent to stir the emotions and engage the will. Preaching seeks to provoke a whole-soul response. A person may be convinced and yet not know a conviction of emotions and will that impel a response. When mind and emotions are engaged the will may be stimulated to action. Timothy Phillips and Denis Okholm state the idea like this, "evangelical apologetics must attend to both reason and rhetoric, with as much emphasis on the latter as the former in order to make reason relevant and help people see the truth." [145]

Proclamation that is unenthusiastic is not only uninteresting but pitiful and preaching that is uninterested in people is pathetic. If preaching is to be persuasive the preacher must be able to identify with the needs of the congregation. If a man is remote and aloof in pastoral ministry and if he is unaware or unconcerned about the welfare of the people then his preaching will have very little impact. That kindred spirit where the man in the pulpit shares the concerns of the congregation in the pews is an important factor in determining how persuasive his preaching will be. If that note of empathy is absent then the majestic melody of preaching will become discordant and cacophonous. What is needed is well prepared sermons that exposit the text, delivered passionately by men of good moral character who identify with the people in the pews. The aim of preaching is not just to get people to comprehend the truth but to embrace it. Tozer makes this point forcefully:

Bible teaching without moral application could be worse than no teaching at all and could result in positive injury to the hearers. What is generally overlooked is that truth as set forth in the Christian Scriptures is a moral thing; it is not addressed to the intellect only, but to the will also. It addresses itself to the total man, and its obligations cannot be discharged by grasping it mentally. Truth engages the citadel of the human heart and is not satisfied until it has conquered everything there.[146]

Truth and application are indivisible and Packer affirms this also, "Preaching is essentially teaching plus application...where the plus is lacking something less than preaching takes place."[147] Broadus agrees, "The application in a sermon is not merely an appendage to the discussion or a subordinate part of it, but is the main thing."[148] Spurgeon was of the same opinion, "Where the application begins, there the sermon begins."[149]

Christians cannot demonstrate with words alone that their faith is "true", no matter how much apologetic emphasis is stressed. McGrath asserts, "When it comes to the big things of life, like believing in the Christian faith or believing in democracy, we live on the basis of probability, not certainty...Christian faith is a risk because it cannot be proven."[150]

Nevertheless, it is the preacher's task to present the Christian message as plausible. Postmodernism rejects the idea of absolute truth, dislikes authority and has cast off all metanarratives, including Christianity, as exploitative. According to this way of thinking Christianity is perceived as a meta-narrative that is proclaimed authoritatively as the absolute truth. This leaves the preacher of Christ with the unenviable and daunting challenge of overcoming such obstacles.

In a postmodern world the mission of Christianity is understood as cultural oppression. Properly understood mission is a holistic one which is much broader than evangelism. It is rooted in the *missio Dei* and as such is God's purpose for the whole of humanity. Mission, therefore, has an ecological dimension which is about stewarding the material resources of creation. It is about serving humanity through development policies and programmes. Yes, it is certainly about bearing witness to the truth but it also has an ethical aspect and, as such, it is about working toward a just society. Moreover it is about being an incarnational community with an intentional missional focus. To reduce mission to evangelism is biblically and theologically incorrect. Furthermore it is intellectually indefensible and as such a *reductio ad absurdum* of the gospel. The polarisation of evangelism, narrowly defined as the proclamation of the truth, and social action, wrongly understood as outside the scope of the gospel is damaging to the cause of the kingdom of God and detracts from the relevance and relational dimension of the gospel.

In the postmodern world where uncertainty and doubt are characteristic traits of thinking, despair is preferable to the deception of worldviews that proselytise for their own self-serving purposes. Graham Johnston argues:

> The issue surrounding the meta-narrative and preaching can come down to the speaker's ethos. Twenty-first-century listeners fear biblical communicator's motives and will question promotion of any particular

worldview. Through humility, love and patience, though, preachers can take measures to dispel the concern of people who have witnessed atrocities and deception in the name of truth and the name of God.[151]

This presents an ethical dimension to the issue of persuasion. The preacher of integrity will not seek to pressurise or manipulate people into making decisions that they do not fully understand. People are suspicious of preachers because they are perceived as silver-tongued orators who entice and entrap needy people to sign up before they develop a sense of scepticism. This wariness of the seductive charms of preachers is part of the cynicism of this generation and the problem is compounded by "preachers" who delude and beguile, often with mesmerising methods, for the purpose of financial gain.[152] There is a moral obligation on those seeking to preach Christ to carefully explain the meaning and implications of faith. When this is done with passion, in the power of the Holy Spirit, by men of integrity who expect that Word to work efficaciously in the hearts of their hearers it can be very persuasive. The Christian communicator is not marketing a product or trying to soft-soap, sugar-coat or sell to potential consumers. Persuasive preaching is not about trying to clinch deals. Nevertheless, it is as Christ's ambassadors that preachers implore others, on Christ's behalf, to be reconciled to God (2 Corinthians 5:20). Packer addresses this matter of importance:

> Far too many pulpit discourses have been put together on wrong principles...Some have expounded biblical doctrine without applying it, thus qualifying as lectures rather than preachments (for lecturing aims only to clear the head, while preaching seeks to change the life); some have been no more than addresses focusing the present self-awareness of the listeners, but not at any stage confronting them with the Word of God...such discourses are less than preaching...but because they were announced as sermons they are treated as preaching and people's idea of preaching gets formed in terms of them, so that the true conception of preaching is forgotten.[153]

The Christian message is perceived by postmodernists as another manipulative metanarrative like, Marxism, Capitalism, Islam, Judaism etc. If Christianity is different in some critical way then the postmodern perception may be disproved. At a superficial level Christianity may appear to be a conventional, controlling metanarrative but the gospel has conspicuous characteristics that would appear to contradict the postmodern view that all metanarratives involve dominance by a preferred group. Marxism, for instance, might be said to be an attractive ideology for the oppressed worker toiling endlessly for the benefit of those who control economic resources. Although it is an ideology that might appeal to the factory worker and the supermarket employee, it will repel the factory owner and the supermarket owner. It is essentially about shifting the balance of power, wealth and privilege and as such it is understood by the dominant economic group to be a threat.

Jesus does not merely present an alternative worldview to dispossess the controlling elite. Rather, his message offered a new paradigm to empower those on the fringes of society, the excluded and the rejected. He did confront the institutional authority of the religious elite with regard to their hypocrisy. He did not, however, reject Nicodemus, a Pharisee and member of the Jewish ruling council, who came to Jesus at night.[154] It was not only members of the religious establishment that were received by Christ. Others such as the despised tax collectors were public officials working for the Roman oppressor and they too were received by Jesus. Christ did not stand for any particular class; rather he included those at the core and those on the periphery. Middleton and Walsh say:

> This radical embrace was vivid testimony to his trust in the Creator of both centre and margins, a Creator who is able to bring life out of even death. The person of Jesus and even his death on a cross, thus becomes in the New Testament a symbol of the counter-ideological intent of the metanarrative and the paradigm or model of ethical human action, even in the face of massive injustice.[155]

But it is not possible to get away from the fact that preaching Christ involves conveying a message. The following list gives a broad outline of the scope of preaching themes: his deity, pre-existence, Trinitarian nature, incarnation, sinless life, public ministry, teaching, death, atonement, resurrection, ascension, glorification, intercessory ministry on behalf of his followers. Then there are his attributes: humility, authority, holiness, power, immutability, transcendence, omnipotence, omniscience, omnipresence and truth. Not only that, but there are a host of themes regarding Christian living and the moral implications and practical application of messages. From this brief glance it may be understood that preaching involves the communication of the central tenets of faith and cherished doctrines enshrined in constitutions and creeds. It is clear that, after all, preaching involves expositing Scripture. Kaiser quotes Bengel, who in 1742 observed:

> Scripture is the foundation of the Church: the Church is the guardian of Scripture. When the Church is in strong health, the light of Scripture shines bright; when the Church is sick, Scripture is corroded by neglect; and thus it happens, that the outward form of Scripture and that of the Church, usually

seem to exhibit simultaneously either health or else sickness; and as a rule the way in which Scripture is being treated is in exact correspondence with the condition of the Church[156]

Kaiser himself goes on to say:

After more than two centuries we can affirm the validity of Bengel's warning. The Church and the Scripture stand or fall together. Either the Church will be nourished and strengthened by the bold proclamation of her Biblical texts or her health will be severely impaired."[157]

A point reinforced by one of today's greatest expository preachers, John Piper, "Where the Bible is esteemed as the inspired and inerrant Word of God, preaching can flourish. But where the Bible is treated merely as a record of valuable religious insight, preaching dies."[158] The notion of persuasive preaching, therefore, when reconceived in classical terms, as distinct from modernist terms, is germane in postmodern culture. Another crucial element in preaching Christ in a postmodern context is that of humility. In a culture where certitude is seen as arrogance, humility is attractive. But humility must be rightly understood.

xv) Humility

Humility should be the hallmark of a preacher, as it was an essential element in the ministry of Christ. Andrew Murray wrote:

If humility is the root of the tree, its nature must be seen in every branch, leaf and fruit. If humility is the first, the all-inclusive grace of the life of Jesus, the secret of his atonement-then the health and strength of our own spiritual life will entirely depend upon our putting this grace first, too. We must make humility the chief thing we admire in Him, the chief thing we ask of Him, the one thing for which we sacrifice all else.[159]

Postmodernism is a profoundly complex "philosophy" or "mood" with significant implications for all religious thought processes including Christian theology. Still in emergent form it is not clear if the postmodern mentality will be more receptive (than the modern mentality) to the idea of preaching Christ. If there is greater optimism about receptivity to Christ in postmodern culture it is counterbalanced by less confidence in preaching as the primary method of reaching the un-churched.

When the apostle Paul spoke about the resurrection of the dead in Athens the text says that, "some of them sneered".[160] This disdainful attitude was also a characteristic of the logical positivism that has dominated thought processes over the past three centuries. But this view has weakened significantly and postmodernity views the universe as a vast space where anything may be possible, including the resurrection. There is a new humility in science. There is less arrogance and a greater hesitancy about making absolute scientific pronouncements. In the context of this new openness postmodern people no longer speak of the world as a self-regulating machine that is programmed to work in accordance with strict natural laws. There is a more humble acknowledgement that the universe is far more complex than previously understood by the scientific community and that it is more like a living organism than a machine. This recognition of the interconnectedness of all things is a feature of postmodernism and is a window of opportunity for the preacher.

For truth to be conveyed effectively there must be some connection between speaker and listener. In a postmodern culture it is better to move away from the term "speaker and listener" because preaching in this context has to be a dialogue rather than a monologue and this "dialogue" is likely to be more than the interchange of opinions at an intellectual or cognitive level. The biblical communicator needs humility (not the same as "hesitancy") in communicating truth with authority. The Puritan, John Flavel said, "a crucified style best suits the preacher of a crucified Christ."[161] This sentiment is supported by John Piper:

> ...the cross is the power of God to crucify the pride of both the preacher and the congregation. In the New Testament the cross is not only a past place of objective substitution; it is also a present place of subjective execution—the execution of my self-reliance and love affair with the praise of men.[162]

The Migliore phrase, "Faith Seeking Understanding", may be helpful in enabling the preacher to identify with non-believers who are also engaged in the same activity.[163] It is important for preachers to retain an interrogative spirit as a safeguard against becoming too doctrinaire. Graham Johnston notes, "The preacher who demonstrates humility with regard to his...own subjective foibles as human interpreter offers a reassuring message to those suspicious of demagoguery."[164]

In preaching frail, flawed and feeble people bear witness to the perfect deity. It is not an arrogant presumption on the part of the preacher to speak of a God who is almighty and perfectly holy, loving and just because the preacher is called to the task by his people and commissioned by God to exercise the function of that office faithfully. As such preaching is not an act of arrogance but of humility.

This draws attention to the manner and practice of preaching which requires humility. But humility can be misplaced, as G. K. Chesterton observed:

> What we suffer from today is humility in the wrong place. Modesty has moved from the organ of ambition. Modesty has settled on the organ of conviction, where it was never meant to be. A man was meant to be doubtful about himself, but undoubting about the truth; this has been exactly reversed. We are on the road to producing a race of men too mentally modest to believe in the multiplication table.[165]

The humility of the messenger is important but this does not necessitate humility regarding the message. The message of Scripture must be proclaimed with a confidence appropriate to its significance and magnitude. James Stewart says:

> It is always thus in every age the ministers of the living Christ are made— the crushing, paralysing sense of abject worthlessness, the self-esteem broken and rolled in the dust, and then a man rising to his full stature as God's commissioned messenger. 'Chief of sinners', 'least of all saints'- such was Paul's self-estimate; yet with what royal, unqualified authority he proclaimed the word and the will of the Lord.[166]

CONCLUSION

The challenge of preaching in a postmodern culture is great and so are the opportunities. The contemporary circumstances demand that preaching should be provocative, challenging and innovative if it going to be engaging. There are many practical ways in which preachers are adjusting the preaching sails to respond to the massive sea changes. The contemporary preacher ought to facilitate a dynamic encounter with the living God. The sermon should animate the text of Scripture so that it is a dramatic recreation which captivates people's imaginations and engages the minds, emotions and wills of hearers. There must be a symbiosis between preacher and congregation, grounded in meaningful relationship. Relevant preaching will be expository, inductive, vivid, Christ-centred and Spirit-empowered. It will have elements of narrative and be rich in illustrations and strong on application. Preaching must be diverse, surprising and poetic. It must be a respectful dialogue between speaker and listener, which is potentially transformative. What is needed more than anything today is preaching which is prophetic, pastoral, powerful and persuasive. Clearly this is a demanding list of expectations which suggests that preaching is indeed a high calling which requires a special anointing of the Holy Spirit. The job of the preacher is to arouse, sustain and satisfy curiosity about the things of God as a means of engaging people in understanding the great disclosure in Scripture.

We cannot ignore postmodernism and we cannot embrace it but we can respond positively to the problems and possibilities it presents. Preachers should be encouraged to preach in a way that demonstrates preaching is more relevant and urgent than ever. It is imperative that the church continues to preach and that preaching is compelling. Some might suggest that the term "preaching" should be abandoned because of its negative connotations. I am not convinced that there is a better word to replace it that would not change the meaning of the function. There is much that can be done to enable hearers to engage with the message (especially by way of using vivid imagery and storytelling) that remains faithful to the Word. Preaching is not just qualitatively different to teaching, it is essentially different. Teaching is a communication process about God but preaching is a process of communion with God.

i) Vox Pop and vanishing pulpits

Authoritative proclamation is disdained in postmodern culture. "Preaching" is a word that is despised. We live in a world where the media does not seem to know the difference between what is in the public interest and what the public is interested in. Is the church any better? What is in the best interest of the church may not, necessarily, be the same thing as what the church is most interested in. It appears that a growing number of churches desire to fulfil a perceived need for the emotional gratification of their congregations rather than exalting the Saviour, evangelising sinners and edifying saints. The church is influenced by the market-driven economy in which we live, where packaging may even take priority over the product. Is the substance of the excellent and efficacious message of the gospel becoming subordinate to the symbolic presentation of that message?

Ideas of truth and revelation are under attack in postmodern society. But God disclosed his message in words. What was once a place of pulpits and pews is becoming a place of soapboxes and sofas, where, in extreme cases, puppeteers are preferred to pastors and preachers! Some might argue that the form or context in which truth is conveyed is irrelevant to the content of that truth but that is a poor judgement. Norrington is correct in stating that, "the sermon is not the only form of discourse which may be inspired by God"[1] This can be readily acknowledged but his argument that the sermon should play a less prominent part in the growing to maturity of the church opens the way for alternatives that ultimately diminish the vitality of the church.

The picture is a sad one where preachers, men with theological understanding, are being constrained by styles of services that require them to fashion performances rather than biblically informed, content-laden preaching. There is a move toward certain kinds of ecclesiology which are entertainment based and in such contexts content is subordinated and sermons are beginning to sound more and more like pithy T-shirt slogans. The danger in mixing the gospel with gimmicks is that people may prefer the gimmicks. Paul's caution to Timothy seems particularly appropriate, "For the time is coming when people will not endure sound teaching, but having itching ears they will accumulate for themselves teachers to suit their own passions." (2 Timothy 4: 3).

In some churches now the scene is set with a certain kind of music that determines what kinds of emotions are to be elicited, which, incidentally, is a standard theatrical device. Though there may not be an overt intention to manipulate, this is, nevertheless, the net effect. It is naive to think that styles of worship are neutral as each style has an agenda of its own, which, sadly, is often not so much about worshipping God as affirming identity. Traditional churches emphasise doctrine and elevate theology. This is good if it is not merely a sentimental attachment to tradition. On the other hand charismatic churches emphasise experience. This is also good as preaching should facilitate a dynamic encounter with the living God. However there is the danger that it will be just an emotional catharsis. The subliminal song in the cabaret church is, "Let Me Entertain You."

Whatever kind of ecclesiology people engage they must follow where the medium leads. Acts 2:42 gives a picture, not only of what the early church was like but what the church ought to be like today. It was not just the norm for then and there it is meant to be normative in the here and now, "And they devoted themselves to the apostles' teaching and the fellowship, to the breaking of bread and the prayers". The medium is abandoned first and then the message.

Many churches have moved towards a different way of conducting business that does not involve preaching, at least as a discreet event in the context of a service. Perhaps this is a reflection of what is happening in society where the nature of discourse has changed. In education, for example, the line of demarcation between learner and teacher is becoming increasingly blurred. Postmodern pedagogy asserts that people can all learn from each other, which is true in itself, but when that view displaces expertise and didactic teaching it is a different matter altogether. Gilbert T. Sewall says:

> Old-time English grammar and Euclidean geometry are not feel-good subjects. They smack of tradition, and they have standards that are easy to measure. Facts, spelling, rules, all demand rote learning, to which many Friere-inspired 'critical thinking' advocates are allergic. They have traded knowledge for forms of inquiry based on feeling, not fact, and on principles based on an intellectual hall of mirrors, stressing perspective, relativity, illusion, and the 'social construction of knowledge'.[2]

The egalitarian spirit that pervades education invites participants to *explore* issues rather than have them *explained*. This subtle change in the use of language indicates shifts in thinking. There is something important in *how* people learn. If, for example, there are open times of sharing people learn that everybody's perspective has equal validity in that kind of egalitarian setting. If, on the other hand the style of teaching is didactic (preaching) we learn that the person speaking has authority. So the context in which a message is experienced is important. A didactic style of preaching presupposes not only that there is a body of doctrine but that there is a structure of authority in communicating it.

It is a sad reality that many churches prefer trivia to theology. One might assume that time constraints prohibit preaching but this is not so as "alternatives" are allocated a considerable amount of time. Instead of, for example, a thirty-minute sermon there are often fragmented messages within a "worship" context. It is naive to suppose that the essence of preaching can be expressed in another way without significantly altering the meaning of the message. This is true of all forms of discourse. If the style of communication is not authoritative proclamation then the message will not be the same. Similarly, if we tone down the demands of the gospel to make it more palatable it becomes something else altogether.

So the preacher is under pressure to keep everything brief and not overtax the attention but to provide constant stimulation through variety and novelty. Bite sized messages are favoured and complexity must be avoided. So exposition is disdained in favour of simple messages. Ultimately this produces emotionally stimulated but biblically illiterate congregations. This is the unintentional and inevitable result of a trivial approach to theology. Brevity does not always suggest triviality but it is not possible to convey the import and implications of the biblical text without adequate time. Consistency and continuity of content may make up for something but will not adequately provide the spiritual nourishment needed in the long term.

In the commercial world there is a significant difference between *product* research and *market* research. The balance has shifted in favour of the latter and the church seems to have followed this pattern. The preacher's product is the Bible and it is to this that he must give attention. But many have begun to look to the market and say what do people want and let's give them that instead. Instead of making sermons of value some preachers are engaged in making the congregation (consumers) feel valuable. Preaching has, therefore, become pseudo psychotherapy in the overall drama of the service. The psychological need of the hearers is paramount rather than the Word of God.

Enjoyment is taken, first as a means to an end and then as an end in itself. So congregations are led to expect to be emotionally stimulated and reject anything that does not deliver this as worthless. Systematic teaching, however, lays a foundation and constructs an edifice and this takes time and commitment on both the parts of the preacher and the hearer. It also assumes that the *growth* of the hearer is paramount. But where the *contentment* of the hearer is of greater importance the message must be made to be immediately accessible and pleasing. There is a pressure to increase stimulation at the expense of education and in the absence of exposition entertainment is the result. In expository preaching the curriculum is the Bible and the purpose is to influence, teach, train and cultivate Christian character by leading people to faith, wholeness and maturity in Christ so that God may be glorified.

Some people seem to think that sermons can be put into Tweets of approximately 150 characters. This is not preaching to a postmodern generation. If it was it would constitute the most outrageous example of dumbing down. It can certainly be a supplement to preaching but it should not supplant it. Admittedly this and Facebook wall messages are valuable means of communicating and networking. In evangelistic terms, perhaps, they are the contemporary equivalent of tract distribution. Twitter has altered some people's approach to theology and preaching but this is ludicrous. Although it may stimulate people to think and be spiritually productive, Tweeting and Twittering is not preaching. It has a place in the ongoing conversation but preaching is an activity that takes place in the context of a gathered community of people committed to interdependent relationships under the authority of biblical leadership not in the individualistic and virtual web of casual connections.

ii) Reviewing the Resurrection (Luke 24:36-43)

The resurrection is something to be experienced rather than understood and this is important in a postmodern culture. On the evening of the resurrection the apostles were assembled together in an upper room when Jesus appeared. They doubted their sense of sight; the nail-pierced hands and feet, so Christ invited them to handle him so that in doing so they would find that he is not a ghost or merely a figment of their troubled minds. Jesus invites enquiry, observation and decision regarding the reality of his resurrection. In effect Jesus is saying investigate and decide. Many like to question but are not interested in answers. Jesus sanctions the principle of inquiry into the foundations of our religious belief. Jesus stands up to scrutiny in his life, earthly ministry and resurrection. If our intellectual faculties need to be satisfied before we can believe in Christ then so be it, although he reminded Thomas eight days later, "Blessed are those who have not seen and yet have believed." The things of God are spiritually discerned through our faculties. God does not bypass our senses, experience and intellect. They are incorporated into faith but do not constitute faith. These things are limited but they can contribute to understanding of and appreciation for the Christian faith. It is possible to be intellectually convinced, spiritually convicted and yet not be converted to faith in Christ. It is the Spirit of God who quickens the souls of men, women and children and it is the power of the Holy Spirit that regenerates.

When Christ entered that room and encountered the disciples in a state of fear he did not remind them of the testimony of the prophets concerning his death and resurrection. He did not refer to his own predictions and teaching on this matter. He did not allude to the reports of Peter and the women he met at the tomb. He never mentioned the two people he met on the road to Emmaus. Christ did not tell them they have had sufficient proof. Rather he invited the doubting Thomas to use the means of inquiry God had given him in order to be satisfied for himself. Christ treats us as individuals and he treats us with dignity. He understands that what should be sufficient to instil faith may in fact, for some people, not be enough. A time may come in a person's life when they think that what they have been taught in childhood about Jesus is, at best, uncertain. There may be times when a disciple's faith is shaken by some trauma and doubts enter that troubled mind. It is at such times that Christ invites, "Behold my hands and My feet, that it is I Myself. Handle me and see..." He wants us to satisfy ourselves of the truth. If we think that the Christian faith might be a figment of our imaginations then Jesus invites investigation. The Christian faith stands up to scrutiny. We may handle it and see for ourselves that it rests on a basis as sure as other knowledge which is generally accepted.

This is important in a postmodern age because handling Christ is not the same as examining creeds and confessions of faith. It is more than doing a course in apologetics. Accepting the invitation of Christ to "handle" him involves honestly searching to ascertain the validity of his truth claims and to discern and decide for ourselves that the Christian faith makes sense. It can be critiqued because it is solid and it is not something that dissolves under scrutiny. The validity of this Christian message can be tested by the understanding. Even though we are finite and limited we can, nevertheless, appraise this gospel and find it will satisfy our curiosity and critical faculties.

Interestingly for preachers in postmodern culture it should be noted that Jesus did not deny their doubt and he did not indulge it, rather he seeks to dispel it. He did not allow their doubts, fears, unbelief and ignorance to be the centre of things. Rather, Jesus himself moves centre stage. There is a kind of religion today that is not so much about Jesus as it is about the feelings, thoughts and experiences of those who claim the name Christian, where God is a concept that is useful in as far as it helps to illustrate the meaning of those experiences. In such a system self is at the centre and God is at the circumference. But God should be at the centre of Christian religious experience and as people come close and handle they are inspired to say with Thomas, "My Lord and my God!"

But there must be both intellectual satisfaction and faith. Postmodern people can be convinced and changed by the power of the gospel. Faith itself is not what saves but the object of that faith; Jesus. So much religion today would say the object of faith is not important but Christ insists on coming centre stage and invites people to examine the evidence and proclaim him as Lord and God. Jesus was not content to let the disciples dabble in their doubt and interpret their experience without reference to the reality of the resurrection. Jesus still appears in post-resurrection, postmodern culture.

iii) Settle out of court

The preacher in a postmodern culture must not forget the seriousness of the homiletic task. He is an advocate seeking to bring about reconciliation of those estranged from God. In Luke 12:54-13:9 Jesus is encountered speaking to a crowd. He advises them, "When you go with your adversary to the magistrate, make every effort along the way to settle with him, lest he drag you to the judge, the judge deliver you to the officer, and the officer throw you into prison." Jesus is advising people to be reconciled to the magistrate along the way. This is an important theme that must be picked up by contemporary preachers.

In temporal terms an out of court settlement saves cost, embarrassment or more serious consequences. Today court cases are booked in advance so that a certain case will, for example, have a number and be scheduled for hearing before the court on a specified date. To have a case settled out of court is generally thought to be advantageous.

Here, in this text, Jesus is telling people that they are in a dispute with God and that they have to come to a decision about who Jesus is. He is telling them that they know what is right and that they need to do what is right without further equivocation. This was a message, not just for *then* and *them* but it is a message for today and *us*. The message is clear: be reconciled to God now. The consequences of failing to do so will be catastrophic because a day is coming when cases will be heard before the eternal judge in the Supreme Court. Scripture warns, "Behold, now is the favorable time; behold, now is the day of salvation," (2 Corinthians 6:2).

If the matter is allowed to drift it will go to court, evidence will be presented and people will be found guilty. The preacher cannot neglect to tell postmodern people that they cannot afford to leave this issue until they get to the courtroom. If this matter is neglected there can be only one outcome and that is a custodial (eternal) sentence. There are dire consequences for those who reject Christ's terms of settlement. If the preacher neglects to preach this he should not be in ministry at all.

This is a text for today's postmodern culture. The preacher, therefore, must exhort people to "...try hard to be reconciled to him on the way." By nature and practice all people are separated from Christ, we are in dispute with God (Romans 3:23; Isaiah 64:6). The gospel is wonderful, even though we are *all* guilty; for those who acknowledge Jesus Christ as Lord and Saviour their debt has been paid and they have been redeemed and reconciled. They have settled out of court on Christ's terms. Thus the apostle Paul declares: "...if anyone is in Christ, he is a new creation; old things have passed away; behold all things have become new" (2 Corinthians 5:17).

The preacher must proclaim the gospel as Paul did when he said, "...we implore you on Christ's behalf, be reconciled to God" (2 Corinthians 5: 20). Every individual has a case to answer, the hearing is scheduled and all their misdeeds are catalogued in the annals. People are guilty of sins of commission and omission. We have all done wrong and failed to do good when we ought to. We are all guilty of sins in sins in thought, word and deed. Imagine the courtroom clerk telling the judge that the next case has been settled out of court. It has been dealt with and therefore deleted. The Lord has spoken on this matter, "Truly, truly, I say to you, whoever hears my word and believes him who sent me has eternal life. He does not come into judgment, but has passed from death to life." (John 5:24).

The language here is emphatic; the literal meaning of the words actually means that their case will never come up. The case has been struck off because it has been dealt with by Christ at Calvary, "There is therefore now no condemnation to those who are in Christ Jesus" (Romans 8:1).

Preachers must not forget that this is an important and urgent matter. This text calls on people to make every effort to be reconciled on the way. We are all on the way to eternity; journeying to that heavenly court. Nobody knows how much longer they have got on that journey. We are exhorted to "make every effort" because there is opposition. People face antagonism from the world, the flesh and the devil. These forces of opposition join together to prevent that reconciliation and people need to be aware that there is a prosecuting barrister, a big wig called Beelzebub. The world would seek to persuade us that the need to settle our affairs with God is just nonsense and the argument is that even if it is true there is no need to do it now; not when you are so young; there is plenty of time and so on. The flesh tells us we couldn't do it; that we will fail and the devil seeks to undermine God's Word. From the time when Adam was in the Garden of Eden and throughout the centuries he has been saying: "you don't take God literally do you?" Procrastination is the thief of time. Before we know it we are not on the way anymore; we have arrived and it is too late. Preaching that is infused with that sense of importance and urgency will hit the target.

iv) Summary

I trust this has been a helpful assessment and critique of postmodernism. It started with some observations relating to shifts in ecclesiology and identified them as a move beyond contextualization to syncretism. The aim of the project has been to assess of the feasibility of preaching in a postmodern culture which rejects both the idea of absolute truth and authority used as power. It traced the historical and philosophical development of postmodernism and showed that the Enlightenment project is deemed to have failed and Christianity has come to be perceived as an oppressive metanarrative. In a world that is becoming increasingly sceptical and where preaching practitioners are becoming disillusioned I trust this book will offer some guidelines about preaching to postmoderns. In a *relational* age *rationality* is impotent, but I hope I have succeeded in distinguishing between *authoritative* and *authoritarian* preaching, thus allowing hope for the survival of the homiletic task. I am convinced that humility is preferable to certitude in all approaches to preaching. It was necessary, in the light of a radical shift in epistemology to redefine the notion of *persuasion*. I suggest that expository preaching is the best model because it diffuses the charge that the preacher is presenting his own opinions. Furthermore I have advocated an inductive mode of communication as a means of engaging postmodern listeners. This is more dialogical and people are more likely to embark on a voyage of discovery than accept deductive arguments presented as truth. I hope in doing this that I have succeeded in signposting a way forward in the labyrinthine complexity of the new paradigm and demonstrated that the homiletic task is still feasible.

SELECTED BIBLIOGRAPHY

Adams, J. E., *Preaching with Purpose*, Grand Rapids: Baker, 1982.

Allen, Ronald J., *Preaching the Topical Sermon*, Louisville: Westminster John Knox Press, 1992.

Anderson, Walter Truett, *Reality Isn't What It Used To Be: Theatrical Politics, Ready-to-Wear Religion, Global Myths, Primitive Chic, and Other Wonders of the Postmodern World*, San Francisco: Harper & Row, 1990.

Appignanesi, Richard and Chris Garratt, *Introducing Postmodernism*, UK: Icon Books, 2003.

Azurdia, Arturo, *Spirit Empowered Preaching: The Vitality of the Holy Spirit in Preaching*, U.K.: Christian Focus, 1998.

Baillie, John, *The Idea of Revelation in Recent Thought*, New York, Columbia University Press, 1956.

Bartow, Charles L., *God's Human Speech: A Practical Theology of Proclamation*, Grand Rapids: William B. Eerdmans, 1997.

Baucham, Richard, *God and the Crisis of Freedom: Biblical and Contemporary Reflections,* Louisville: Westminster John Knox Press, 2002.

Begg, Alistair, *Preaching for God's Glory*, Wheaton: Crossway Books, 1999.

Bonhoeffer, Deitrich, *Worldly Preaching: Lectures on Homiletics*, trans. Clyde E. Fant, Nashville: Thomas Nelson, 1975.

Brian McLaren and Steve Rabey, *The Church on the Other Side: Doing Ministry in the Postmodern Matrix*, Grand Rapids: Zondervan, 2000.

Broadus, John A., *On the Preparation and Delivery of Sermons*, 4th. ed., revised by Vernon L. Stanfield, San Francisco: Harper & Row, 1979.

Brown, Colin, *Philosophy & the Christian Faith*, London: Tyndale Press, 1968.

Brueggemann, Walter, *An Introduction to the Old Testament: The Canon and Christian Imagination*, Louisville: Westminster John Knox Press, 2003.

Bultmann, Rudolph, *Jesus and the Word*, New York: Scribner Press, 1935.

Buttrick, David, *Homiletic Moves and Structures*, Philadelphia: Fortress Press, 1987.

Caemmerer, Richard R., *Preaching for the Church*, St. Louis: Concordia Publishing House, 1959.

Cahoone, Lawrence, ed. *From Modernism to Postmodernism: An Anthology*, Malden: Blackwell Publishers, 1997.

Capill, Murray A., *Preaching with Spiritual Vigour*, Glasgow: Christian Focus, 2003.

Carson, D. A. (ed.), *Telling the Truth: Evangelising Postmoderns*, Grand Rapids: Zondervan, 2000.

Carson, D. A., *Becoming Conversant with the Emergent Church: Understanding a Movement and Its Implications*, Grand Rapids: Zondervan, 2005.

—. *The Gagging of God: Christianity Confronts Pluralism,* Grand Rapids: Zondervan, 1996.

Chapell, Bryan, *Christ-Centred Preaching*, Grand Rapids: Baker Books, 1994.

Colson, Charles and Nancy Pearcey, *How Now Shall We Live?* Nashville: Lifeway Press, 1999.

Craddock, Fred, *As One Without Authority*, Nashville: Abingdon, 1981.

Dabney, Robert L, *Evangelical Eloquence: A Course of Lectures on Preaching*, Banner of Truth Trust, 1999.

Dargan, Edwin Charles, *A History of Preaching*, Grand Rapids: Baker Book House, 1954.

Davis, H. Grady, *Design for Preaching*, Philadelphia: Fortress Press, 1958.

Derrida, Jacques, *Deconstruction in a Nutshell: A Conversation with Jacques Derrida*, ed. John D. Caputo, New York: Fordham University Press, 1997.

Dockery, David. (ed.) *The Challenge of Postmodernism: An Evangelical Engagement*, Grand Rapids: Baker, 1997 (Previous edition: Wheaton, Ill.: Victor Books, 1995).

Duduit, Michael (ed.) *Handbook of Contemporary Preaching*, Nashville: Broadman Press, 1992.

Eagleton, Terry, *After Theory*, New York, Basic Books, 2003.

—. *Against the Grain,* London: Verso Press, 1986.

—. *Literary Theory,* Oxford, Blackwell, 1983.

Ebeling, Gerhard, *Theology and Proclamation: A Discussion with Rudolf Bultmann*, trans. by John Riches, London: Collins, 1966.

Eby, David, *Power Preaching for Church Growth*, Mentor, 1998.

Erickson, Millard J., *Christian Theology*, Grand Rapids: Baker Books, 1998.

—. *Postmodernizing the Faith: Evangelical Responses to the Challenge of Postmodernism*, 2d ed., Grand Rapids: Baker Books, 1998.

—. *The Postmodern World: Discerning the Times and the Spirit of our Age*, Wheaton, Ill.: Crossway, 2002.

Erickson, Millard, *Truth or Consequences: The Promise and Perils of Postmodernism*, Downers Grove, Ill.: InterVarsity Press, 2001.

Eslinger, Richard L., The *Web of Preaching*, Nashville: Abingdon Press, 2002.

Fabarez, Michael, *Preaching that Changes Lives*, Nashville: Thomas Nelson, 2002.

Fairlamb, Horace L., *Critical Conditions: Postmodernity and the Questions of Foundations*, Cambridge University Press, 1994.

Franke, John R., *The Character of Theology: An Introduction to Its Nature, Task and Purpose*, Grand Rapids: Baker, 2005.

Greidanus, Sidney, *The Modern Preacher and the Ancient Text: Interpreting and Preaching Biblical Literature*, Grand Rapids: Eerdmans, and Leicester: Inter-Varsity Press 1988 (reprinted 1996).

Grenz, Stanley J., *A Primer on Postmodernism*, Grand Rapids: William B. Eerdmans, 1996.

Grenz, Stanley, and John R. Franke, *Beyond Foundationalism: Shaping Theology in a Postmodern Context*, Louisville: Westminster: John Knox Press, 2001.

Griffin, David Ray, William A. Beardslee, and Joe Holland, eds. *Varieties of Postmodern Theology*, Albany, NY: SUNY Press, 1989.

Groothuis, Douglas, *Truth Decay: Defending Christianity Against the Challenges of Postmodernism*, Downers Grove, Illinois: InterVarsity Press, 2000.

Guinness, Os, *Dining with the Devil*, Grand Rapids: Baker, 1993.

Harvey, David, *The Condition of Postmodernity: An Enquiry into the Origins of Cultural Change*, Cambridge Mass: Blackwell, 1989.

Heflin, James and Millard Erickson, *Old Wine in New Wineskins: Doctrinal Preaching in a Changing World*, Grand Rapids: Baker Books, 1997.

Hilborn, David, *Picking Up the Pieces: Can Evangelicals Adapt to Contemporary Culture?* London: Hodder and Stoughton, 1997.

Honderich, Ted (ed.) *The Oxford Companion to Philosophy*, Oxford University Press, 1995.

Hughes, Jack, *Expository Preaching with Word Pictures*, Ross-shire: Christian Focus, 2001.

Johnston, Graham, *Preaching To A Postmodern World*, Leicester: Inter-Varsity Press, 2001.

Kaiser, Walter C. Jr., *Toward an Exegetical Theology: Biblical Exegesis for Preaching and Teaching,* Grand Rapids: Baker Book House, 1981, (twelfth printing 1996).

Kaufman, Gordon D., *God the Problem,* Cambridge: Harvard University Press, 1972.

Kimball, Dan, *The Emerging Church: Vintage Christianity for New Generations,* Grand Rapids: Zondervan, 2003.

Lakeland, Paul, *Postmodernity: Christian Identity in a Fragmented Age,* Minneapolis: Fortress Press, 1997, x-xi.

Larsen, C. F. David, *The Company of Preachers: A History of Biblical Preaching from the Old Testament to the Modern Era,* Grand Rapids: Kregel, 1998.

Larsen, David L., *Telling the Old, Old Story, The Art of Narrative Preaching,* Kregel Academic and Professional, 2001.

Lewis, L., and Lewis, G., *Inductive Preaching,* Illinois: Crossway, 1983.

Lewis, L., and Lewis, G., *Learning to Preach Like Jesus,* Illinois: Crossway, 1989.

Lewis, Ralph L. and Gregg Lewis, *Inductive Preaching: Helping People Listen,* Westchester, Ill.: Crossway Books, 1983.

Liefeld, W. L., *New Testament Exposition: From Text to Sermon,* Grand Rapids: Zondervan, 1984.

Lindbeck, George, A., *The Nature of Doctrine: Religion and Theology in a Postliberal Age,* Philadelphia: Westminster John Knox, 1984.

Lischer, Richard, *A Theology of Preaching: The Dynamics of the Gospel,* Durham: The Labyrinth Press, 1992.

Lloyd-Jones, Martyn, *Preaching and Preachers,* Grand Rapids: Zondervan, 1971.

Logan, Samuel T. (ed.), *The Preacher and Preaching: Reviving the Art in the Twentieth Century,* Darlington and Phillipsburg, P and R Publishing Company, 1986.

Long, Thomas, *Narrative Structure as Applied to Biblical Preaching,* University Microfilms International, 1980.

—. *Preaching and the Literary Form of the Bible,* Philadelphia: Fortress Press, 1989.

—. *The Witness of Preaching,* Louisville: John Knox Press, 1989.

Louw, Johannes P., and Eugene A. Nida, *Greek-English Lexicon of the New Testament,* Bible Society of South Africa, 1989.

Lowry, Eugene L., *The Homiletical Plot: the Sermon as Narrative Art Form,* Atlanta: John Knox Press, 1980.

Lowry, Eugene, *The Sermon: Dancing the Edge of Mystery,* Nashville: Abingdon Press, 1997.

Lyon, David, *Postmodernity: Concepts in Social Thought*, 2nd ed. Minneapolis: University of Minnesota Press, 1999.

Lyotard, Jean Francois, *The Postmodern Condition: A Report on Knowledge*, Minneapolis: University of Minnesota Press, 1984.

Mayhue, Richard L. (ed.), *Rediscovering Expository Preaching*, Mayhue, Dallas: Word, 1992.

McCallum, Dennis (ed.) *The Death of Truth*, Minneapolis: Bethany House, 1996.

McCullough, Donald W., *The Trivialization of God: The Dangerous Illusion of A Manageable Deity*, Colorado Springs: Nav Press, 1995.

McGrath, Alister, *Bridge-Building: Effective Christian Apologetics*, Leicester, England: IVP, 1992.

—. *Christian Theology*, 2d ed., Malden: Blackwell Publishers, 1998.

McLaren, Brian, *The Church on the Other Side: Doing Ministry in the Postmodern Matrix*, Grand Rapids: Zondervan, 2000.

Middleton, Richard and Brian J. Walsh, *Truth is Stranger than it Used to Be: Biblical Faith in a Postmodern Age*, Downers Grove, Ill.: InterVarsity, 1995.

Migliore, Daniel L., *Faith Seeking Understanding: An Introduction to Christian Theology*, Grand Rapids: Michigan, Eerdmans, 1991.

Murray, Andrew, *Humility*, New Kensington: Pa.: Whitaker House, 1982.

Nash, Ronald H., *The Word of God and the Mind of Man*, Phillipsburg: P & R Publishing, 1982.

Netland, Harold, *Encountering Religious Pluralism: The Challenge to Christian Faith & Mission*, Downers Grove, Ill: InterVarsity, 2001.

Norris, Christopher, *The Truth About Postmodernism*, Cambridge: Blackwell, 1993.

Oden, Thomas C., *After Modernity...What? Agenda for Theology*, Grand Rapids: Zondervan, 1990.

—. *Two Worlds: Notes on the Death of Modernity in America and Russia*, Downers Grove, Ill.: InterVarsity Press, 1992

Oliver, Martyn, *History of Philosophy: Great Thinkers from 600 B.C. to the Present Day*, New York: Barnes and Noble Books, 1999.

Perkins, William, *The Art of Prophesying*, Edinburgh: Banner of Truth, 1996.

Phillips, Timothy R. and Dennis L. Ockholm, *Christian Apologetics in the Postmodern World*, Downers Grove: InterVarsity Press, 1995.

Pieterse, H. J. C., *Communicative Preaching*, Pretoria: University of South Africa, 1987.

Piper, John, *The Supremacy of God in Preaching,* Grand Rapids: Baker House Books, 1990.

Plantinga, Alvin, *Warranted Christian Belief*, New York: OUP, 2000.

Pojman, Louis P., *What Can We Know? An Introduction to the Theory of Knowledge*, Belmont, CA: Wadsworth/Thomas Learning, 2001.

Polluck, John L., and Joseph Cruz, *Contemporary Theories of Knowledge*, Landham, Maryland: Rowman & Littlefield, 1999.

Rabey, Steve, *In Search of Authentic Faith: How Emerging Generations are Transforming the Church*, Colorado Springs: Waterbook Press, 2001.

Rabinow, Paul, (ed.), *Foucault Reader*, New York: Pantheon, 1984.

Reymond, Robert L., *The God-Centred Preacher,* Glasgow: Christian Focus, 2003.

Robinson, Haddon W., *Biblical Preaching: The Development and Delivery of Expository Messages*, Grand Rapids: Baker, 1980.

Robinson, W. B., *Journeys Toward Narrative Preaching*, New York: Pilgrim Press, 1990.

Rorty, Richard, *Philosophy and the Mirror of Nature*, Princeton N.J.: Princeton University Press, 1979.

Rose, Lucy Atkinson, *Sharing the Word: Preaching in the Roundtable Church*, Westminster: John Knox Press, 1997.

Sangster, William E., *The Craft of Sermon Construction*, reprint, Grand Rapids: Baker Book House, 1972.

Sargent, Tony, *The Sacred Anointing*, Wheaton: Crossway Books, 1994.

Schaeffer, Francis A., *Escape from Reason*, in *The Complete Works of Francis A. Schaeffer*, vol. 1, *A Christian View of Philosophy and Culture*, Westchester Ill.: Crossway Books, 1982.

Schlafer, D. J., *Surviving the Sermon*, 1992, Cambridge: Cowley Publications, 63, 68-70.

Schleiermacher, Friedrich, *On Religion: Addresses in Response to its Cultural Critics*, Richmond: John Knox Press, 1969.

—. *The Christian Faith,* translated from the second German edition, ed. H. R. Mackintosh and J. S. Steward, Edinburgh: T & T Clark, 1928.

Spurgeon, Charles Haddon, *Lectures to my Students*, Grand Rapids: Zondervan, 1970 (reprinted ed., Pasadena: Pilgrim Publications, 1990).

Stewart, James S., *Heralds of God: A Practical Book on Preaching*, Regent College Publishing, 1946.

Stott, John, *Between Two Worlds: The Art of Preaching in the Twentieth Century*, Grand Rapids: William B. Eerdmans, 1982.

—. *I Believe in Preaching*, London: Hodder and Stoughton, 1982.

Sweet, Leonard D., *Carpe Manana*, Grand Rapids: Zondervan, 2001.

—. *Postmodern Pilgrims: First Century Passion for the 21st Century World*, Nashville: Broadman & Holman, 2000.

—. *Soul Tsunami*, Grand Rapids: Zondervan, 1999.

Sweet, Leonard, Brian McLaren and Jerry Haselmayer, *'A' is for Abductive: The Language of the Emerging Church*, Grand Rapids: Zondervan, 2003.

Sweet, Leonard, *Jesus Drives Me Crazy*, Grand Rapids: Zondervan, 2003.

Tarnas, Richard, *The Passion of the Western Mind: Understanding the Ideas That Have Shaped Our World Views*, New York: Ballantine Books, 1991.

Temple, William, *Nature, Man and God*, New York, St Martin's Press, 1934.

Unger, Merril F., *The Principles of Expository Preaching*, Grand Rapids: Zondervan, 1955.

Vanhoozer, Kevin J. (ed.) *The Cambridge Companion to Postmodern Theology*, Cambridge: Cambridge University Press, 2003.

—. *First Theology: God, Scripture and Hermeneutics*, Leicester: Apollos, 2002.

—. *Is There a Meaning in This Text?* Grand Rapids: Zondervan, 1998.

—. *The Drama of Doctrine*, Louisville: Westminster John Knox Press, 2005.

Veith, Gene Edward Jr., *Postmodern Times: A Christian Guide to Contemporary Thought and Culture*, Wheaton, Illinois: Crossway, 1994.

Von Rad, G., *Biblical Interpretations in Preaching*, Nashville: Abingdon, 1977.

Vos, C. J. A., (ed.), *Proclaim the Gospel*, Pretoria: Etiole, 1994.

Vos, C. J. A., *Theopoetry in the Psalms*, Pretoria: Protea Book House, 2005.

Ford, David F. (ed.) *The Modern Theologians*, Malden: Blackwell Publishers, 1997.

Waugh, Patricia, *Postmodernism: A Reader*, London: Edward Arnold, 1992.

Wells, David F., *God in the Wasteland*, Leicester: Inter-Varsity Press, 1994.

—. *No Place for Truth, Or Whatever Happened to Evangelical Theology?* Grand Rapids: William B. Eerdmans, 1993.

NOTES

CHAPTER ONE: THE SHIFT FROM CONTEXTUALIZATION TO SYNCRETISM IN THE WESTERN CHRISTIAN CHURCH

[1] Moreau, A. Scott. "Contextualization: From an Adapted Message to an Adapted Life", *The Changing Face of World Missions*, by Michael Pocock, Gailyn Van Rheenen, and Douglas McConnell, Grand Rapids: Baker Academic, 2005, 321-348.

[2] Carson, Don A. "Church and Mission: Reflections on Contextualization and the Third Horizon", *The Church in the Bible and the World: An International Study*, ed. D. A. Carson, Grand Rapids: Baker, 1987, 219-220.

[3] Carson, Don A., "Church and Mission: Reflections on Contextualization and the Third Horizon", 219-220.

[4] Van Rheenen, Gailyn, "Modern and Postmodern Syncretism in Theology and Missions", *The Holy Spirit and Mission Dynamics*, ed. C. Douglas McConnell, Pasadena: Wm. Carey, 1997, 173.

[5] Van Rheenen, Gailyn, "Modern and Postmodern Syncretism in Theology and Missions", 173.

[6] Groothuis, Douglas, "Facing the Challenge of Postmodernism", *To Everyone and Answer :A Case for the Christian Worldview*, Francis Beckwith, William Lane Craig and J. P. Moreland (eds.), Downers Grove, Illinois: IVP, 2004, 253.

[7] Stackhouse, John G. Jr., "From Architecture to Argument; Historic Resources for Christian Apologetics" *Christian Apologetics in the Postmodern World*, Timothy R. Phillips and Dennis L. Okholm (eds.), Downers Grove, Illinois: IVP, 1995, 40

[8] Frost, Michael and Alan Hirsch, *The Shaping of Things to Come: Innovation and Mission for the 21st-Century Church,* (published jointly) Peabody, Massachusetts: Hendrickson Publishers and in Australia by Strand Publishing, NSW, 2003, ix.

[9] Frost, Michael and Alan Hirsch, *The Shaping of Things to Come: Innovation and Mission for the 21st-Century Church,* ix.

[10] Of course educationalists must be open to new research and varied approaches and methodologies without recklessly abandoning what have served well for novel approaches where the outcomes are uncertain.

[11] Appignanesi, Richard and Chris Garratt, *Introducing Postmodernism*, UK: Icon Books, 2003, 52.

[12] Growth could be more comprehensively understood as a process whereby individuals grow to maturity and the church community grows together in unity and then grows out to the community. The end result of this process may be a growth in numbers.

[13] The author acknowledges his admiration for Martin Luther King's social, political and religious message and style of communication.

[14] "Prophecy" here is defined as a *fort-telling* of the mind of God through exposition of revelation rather than a *foretelling* of future events.
[15] This is not to say that Colonialism, Capitalism, Nazism and Marxism are morally equivalent.
[16] There will be further brief discussion of the *missio Dei* later.
[17] Bosch, David. *Transforming Mission: Paradigm Shifts in Theology of Mission*, Orbis Books, Maryknoll: New York, 1991, 390
[18] Pachuau, L. "*Missio Dei*", *Dictionary of Missionary Theology: Evangelical Foundations*, Corrie, John (ed.), Nottingham: Inter-Varsity Press, 2007, 234.

CHAPTER TWO: UNDERSTANDING POSTMODERNISM: ISSUES PERTAINING TO THE FEASIBILITY OF THE HOMILETIC TASK IN THE CONTEMPORARY EPISTEMOLOGICAL CONTEXT

[1] Anderson, Walter Truett, *Reality Isn't What It Used To Be: Theatrical Politics, Ready-to-Wear Religion, Global Myths, Primitive Chic, and Other Wonders of the Postmodern World*, San Francisco: Harper & Row, 1990.
Lakeland, Paul, *Postmodernity: Christian Identity in a Fragmented Age*, Minneapolis: Fortress Press, 1997, x-xi.
[2] Guarino, Thomas, "Postmodernity and Five Fundamental Theological Issues", *Theological Studies*, 57, No. 4, December 1996, 654.
[3] Adams, Daniel J., "Toward a Theological Understanding of Postmodernism", *Cross Currents*, 47, No. 4, Winter 97-98, 518.
[4] Cahoone, Lawrence, ed. *From Modernism to Postmodernism: An Anthology,* Malden: Blackwell Publishers, 1997, 1.
[5] Postmodernism is characteristically anti-Western civilisation and opposes what it views as abuses by the West.
[6] Cahoone, Lawrence, *From Modernism to Postmodernism*, 1.
[7] Colson, Charles and Nancy Pearcey, *How Now Shall We Live?* Nashville: Lifeway Press, 1999, 48.
[8] McGrath, Alister, *Christian Theology*, 2d ed., Malden: Blackwell Publishers, 1998, 114.
[9] Cahoone, Lawrence, *From Modernism to Postmodernism*, 1.
[10] Dockery, David. (ed.) *The Challenge of Postmodernism: An Evangelical Engagement*, Grand Rapids: Baker, 1997. Previous edition: Wheaton, Ill.: Victor Books, 1995, 16.
[11] Griffin, David Ray, William A. Beardslee, and Joe Holland, eds. *Varieties of Postmodern Theology*, Albany, NY: SUNY Press, 1989. Some include liberation, feminist, and contemporary Roman Catholic theologies
[12] Tarnas, Richard, *The Passion of the Western Mind: Understanding the Ideas That Have Shaped Our World Views,* New York: Ballantine Books, 1991, 395.
[13] Adams, Daniel J., "Toward a Theological Understanding of Postmodernism", 520; Allen, Diogenes, "The End of the Modern World", *Christian Scholar's Review*, 22, no. 4, 1993, 340.

[14] Adams, Daniel J., "Toward a Theological Understanding of Postmodernism", 520.

[15] Adams, Daniel J., "Toward a Theological Understanding of Postmodernism", 520.

[16] Cahoone, Lawrence, *From Modernism to Postmodernism*, 14.

[17] "The term 'postmodern' primarily refers to time rather than to a distinct ideology." Dockery, David S., "The Challenges of Postmodernism", 13. Ward views postmodernism more as a "condition" than as a period. See: Ward, Graham, "Postmodern Theology", *The Modern Theologians*, ed. David F. Ford, Malden: Blackwell Publishers, 1997, 585. See also: Oliver, Martyn, *History of Philosophy: Great Thinkers from 600 B.C. to the Present Day*, New York: Barnes and Noble Books, 1999, 171, 189.

[18] Griffin, David Ray, William A. Beardslee, and Joe Holland, eds.*Varieties of Postmodern Theology*, xii.

[19] Cahoone, Lawrence, *From Modernism to Postmodernism*, 14.

[20] According to Henry, much that characterised modern theology "carries over into postmodernism's postulations." Henry, Carl F. H., "Postmodernism: The New Spectre?" *The Challenge of Postmodernism: An Evangelical Engagement*, ed. David S. Dockery, Wheaton: Victor Books, 1995, 38. See also: Wells, David F., *No Place for Truth, Or Whatever Happened to Evangelical Theology?* Grand Rapids: William B. Eerdmans, 1993, 61.

[21] Cahoone, Lawrence, *From Modernism to Postmodernism*, 3. According to Grenz, Nietzsche (1844-1900) was the first to attack modernism, "but the full-scale frontal assault did not begin until the 1970s." Grenz, Stanley J., *A Primer on Postmodernism*, Grand Rapids: William B. Eerdmans, 1996, 5. See also: Tarnas, Richard, *The Passion of the Western Mind: Understanding the Ideas That Have Shaped Our World Views*, 395.

[22] Henry, Carl F. H., "Postmodernism: The New Spectre?" 35.

[23] Cahoone, Lawrence, *From Modernism to Postmodernism*, 2. See also McGrath, Alister, *Christian Theology*, 575.

[24] Allen, Diogenes, "The End of the Modern World: A New Openness for Faith", *Princeton Seminary Bulletin*, 11, 1990, 340. Oden, Thomas C., "The Death of Modernity and Postmodern Evangelical Spirituality", *The Challenge of Postmodernism: An Evangelical Engagement*, ed. David S. Dockery, Wheaton: Victor Books, 1995, 24.

[25] McGrath, Alister, *Christian Theology*, 113.

[26] Adams, Daniel J., "Toward a Theological Understanding of Postmodernism", 519. Fairlamb is correct, postmodern scepticism reaches "not only to modernism, but to Western philosophy as a whole." Fairlamb, Horace L., *Critical Conditions: Postmodernity and the Questions of Foundations*, Cambridge University Press, 1994, 1.

[27] McGrath, Alister, *Christian Theology*, 575. According to Christopher Norris, postmodernism "is a 'family resemblance' term deployed in a variety of contexts (architecture, painting, music, poetry, fiction, etc.) for things which seem to be related—if at all—by a laid back pluralism of styles and a vague desire to have done with the pretensions of high modernist culture." Norris, Christopher, "Post-

modernism", *The Oxford Companion to Philosophy*, ed. Ted Honderich, Oxford University Press, 1995, 708.

[28] Veith says, "If the *modern* era is over, we are all postmodern, even though we reject the tenets of postmodernism." Veith, Gene Edward, *Postmodern Times: A Christian Guide to Contemporary Thought and Culture*, Wheaton: Crossway Books, 1994, 42.

[28] Allen, Ronald J., "Preaching and Postmodernism", *Interpretation*, January, 2001.34.

[30] Dockery, David, "The Challenge of Postmodernism", 14.

[31] Dockery, David, "The Challenge of Postmodernism", 14.

[32] Erickson, Millard J., *Christian Theology*, Grand Rapids: Baker Books, 1998, 160. Adams writes, "One cannot speak of the postmodern without first speaking of modernity and modernism." Adams, Daniel J., "Toward a Theological Understanding of Postmodernism", 518.

[33] Erickson, Millard J., *Postmodernizing the Faith: Evangelical Responses to the Challenge of Postmodernism,* 2d ed., Grand Rapids: Baker Books, 1998, 15.

[34] Erickson, Millard J., *Postmodernizing the Faith: Evangelical Responses to the Challenge of Postmodernism*, 15.

[35] Grenz, Stanley J., *A Primer on Postmodernism*, Grand Rapids: Eerdmans, 1996. 61. See also: Grenz, Stanley, and John R. Franke, *Beyond Foundationalism: Shaping Theology in a Postmodern Context*, Louisville: Westminster: John Knox Press, 2001. Also: Franke, John R., *The Character of Theology: An Introduction to Its Nature, Task and Purpose*, Grand Rapids: Baker, 2005.

[36] Erickson, Millard J., *Christian Theology*, 160.

[37] Henry, Carl F., "Postmodernism: The New Spectre?" 36. See Erickson, Millard J. *Christian Theology*, 160.

[38] Erickson, Millard J., *Postmodernizing the Faith*, 15.

[39] Erickson, Millard J., *Christian Theology*, 161.

[40] Allen, Ronald J., "Preaching and Postmodernism", *Interpretation*, 35.

[41] Veith, Gene Edward Jr., *Postmodern Times: A Christian Guide to Contemporary Thought and Culture*. See also: Oden, Thomas C., *Two Worlds: Notes on the Death of Modernity in America and Russia*, Downers Grove, Ill.: InterVarsity Press, 1992, 32. Though Oden uses the term "ultramodernity" rather than "postmodernity", he does argue that a definite cultural shift began at the end of modernity.

[42] Johnston, Graham, *Preaching to a Postmodern World*, Grand Rapids: IVP, 2001, 24.

[43] Brown, Colin, *Philosophy & the Christian Faith*, London: Tyndale Press, 1968, 50.

[44] "Cartesian" here is the adjective which alludes to René Descartes (1596–1650) the French philosopher and mathematician or his philosophy. After a Jesuit education and military service, he settled in Holland. Descartes' Discourse on Method (1637) introduced themes which he developed in his greatest work, the *Meditations* (1641). Asking "How and what do I know?" he arrived at his famous statement "Cogito ergo sum" ("I think, therefore I am"). From this he proved to his own satisfaction God's existence (he was a Roman Catholic) and hence the

existence of everything else. He believed that the world consisted of two different substances—mind and matter (the doctrine of Cartesian dualism). He held that mathematics was the supreme science.

[45] It should be noted that René Descartes had no intention of promoting a philosophical system that excluded God from the equation. In fact, Descartes reasoned from his own existence that a God must exist. See: Brown, Colin, *Philosophy & the Christian Faith*, 51.

[46] Johnston, Graham, *Preaching to a Postmodern World*, 25.

[47] Brown, Colin, *Philosophy & the Christian Faith*, 68.

[48] Pojman, Louis P., *What Can We Know? An Introduction to the Theory of Knowledge*, Belmont, CA: Wadsworth/Thomas Learning, 2001, 16.

[49] The term "modern scepticism" is used to differentiate it from ancient scepticism that goes back at least as far as Socrates who frequently began an enquiry: "We ought to investigate this." The Greek word means to enquire or investigate. See: Pojman, Louis P., *What Can We Know An Introduction to the Theory of Knowledge*, 27.

[50] Polluck, John L., and Joseph Cruz, *Contemporary Theories of Knowledge*, Landham, Maryland: Rowman & Littlefield, 1999, 2.

[51] In postmodernism, "scepticism" has been replaced with "suspicion".

[52] Veith, Gene Edward Jr., *Postmodern Times: A Christian Guide to Contemporary Thought and Culture*, 35-36.

[53] Veith, Gene Edward Jr., *Postmodern Times: A Christian Guide to Contemporary Thought and Culture*, 37.

[54] Veith, Gene Edward Jr., *Postmodern Times: A Christian Guide to Contemporary Thought and Culture*, 37.

[54] Brown, Colin, *Philosophy and the Christian Faith*, 129.

[56] Veith, Gene Edward Jr., *Postmodern Times: A Christian Guide to Contemporary Thought and Culture*, 35.

[57] Veith, Gene Edward Jr., *Postmodern Times: A Christian Guide to Contemporary Thought and Culture*, 35.

[58] Brown, Colin, *Philosophy and the Christian Faith*, 91.

[59] Brown, Colin, *Philosophy and the Christian Faith*, 96.

[60] Schaeffer, Francis A., *Escape from Reason*, in *The Complete Works of Francis A. Schaeffer*, vol. 1, *A Christian View of Philosophy and Culture*, Westchester Ill.: Crossway Books, 1982, 233.

[61] Schaeffer, Francis A., *Escape from Reason*, in *The Complete Works of Francis A. Schaeffer*, 233.

[62] Schaeffer, Francis A., *Escape from Reason*, in *The Complete Works of Francis A. Schaeffer*, 237.

[63] Plantinga, Alvin, *Warranted Christian Belief*, New York: OUP, 2000, 422-423. See also: Erickson, Millard J., *The Postmodern World: Discerning the Times and the Spirit of our Age*, Wheaton, Ill.: Crossway, 2002, 117.

[64] Henry, Carl F., "Postmodernism: The New Spectre?" 37.

[65] Grenz, Stanley J., *A Primer on Postmodernism*, 2-3.

[66] Tarnas, Richard., *The Passion of the Western Mind*, 279.

[67] Carson, D. A., *The Gagging of God: Christianity Confronts Pluralism,* Grand Rapids: Zondervan, 1996, 61.

[68] Henry, Carl F., "Postmodernism: The New Spectre?" 37.

[69] As Henry notes, "The intellectual order of the world was relocated in human reasoning. This control over nature and history would free humankind from...a predetermined universe." Henry, Carl F., "Postmodernism: The New Spectre?" 36.

[70] Locke, John, *An Essay Concerning Human Understanding,* ed. Peter H. Nidditch, Oxford: Oxford University Press, 1975, 704.

[71] Baucham, Richard, *God and the Crisis of Freedom: Biblical and Contemporary Reflections,* Louisville: Westminster John Knox Press, 2002.

[72] Oden, Thomas C., "The Death of Modernity and Postmodern Evangelical Spirituality" 24.

[73] Jones, O. R., "Foundationalism", *The Oxford Companion to Philosophy,* ed. Ted Honderich, Oxford: Oxford University Press, 1995, 289.

[74] Carson, D. A., *The Gagging of God,* 61.

[75] Carson, D. A., *The Gagging of God,* 59-60. Carson points out that, "this quest for certainty was supported by seminal thinkers like Locke, Kant, and Hegel; it reached out to embrace almost every discipline", 60.

[76] Carson, D. A., *The Gagging of God,* 63.

[77] Cahoone, Lawrence, *From Modernism to Postmodernism,* 482, fn.1. See also: Waugh, Patricia, *Postmodernism: A Reader,* London: Edward Arnold, 1992, 1.

[78] Lyotard, Jean-Francois, "The Postmodern Condition: A Report on Knowledge", *From Modernism to Postmodernism,* Minneapolis: University of Minnesota Press, 1984, 482.

[79] Carson, D. A., *The Gagging of God,* 63.

[80] McGrath, Alister, *Christian Theology,* 113.

[81] Anderson, Walter Truett. *Reality Isn't What It Used To Be: Theatrical Politics, Ready-to-Wear Religion, Global Myths, Primitive Chic, and Other Wonders of the Postmodern World,* 5. Carl F. Henry points out that many thinkers are convinced that postmodernism has "the status of a major irreversible movement." Henry, Carl F., "Postmodernism: The New Spectre?" 35.

[82] Anderson, Walter Truett, *Reality Isn't What It Used To Be: Theatrical Politics, Ready-to-Wear Religion, Global Myths, Primitive Chic, and Other Wonders of the Postmodern World,* 5.

[83] Anderson, Walter Truett, *Reality Isn't What It Used To Be: Theatrical Politics, Ready-to-Wear Religion, Global Myths, Primitive Chic, and Other Wonders of the Postmodern World,* 5.

[84] Oden, Thomas C., "So What Happens after Modernity? A Postmodern Agenda for Evangelical Theology", *The Challenge of Postmodernism: An Evangelical Engagement,* ed. David. Dockery, 395. See also: Henry, Carl F., "Postmodernism: The New Spectre?" 40.

[85] Oden, Thomas C., "So What Happens after Modernity?" 395.

[86] Carson, D. A., *Becoming Conversant with the Emergent Church: Understanding a Movement and Its Implications,* Grand Rapids: Zondervan, 2005, 78.

[87] Carson, D. A., *Becoming Conversant with the Emergent Church,* 79.

[88] McGrath, Alister, *Christian Theology,* 114

[89] Carson, D. A., *The Gagging of God*, 100.
[90] Miller, James B., "The Emerging Postmodern World," *Postmodern Theology: Christian Faith in a Pluralist World*, ed. Frederic B. Burnham, San Francisco: Harper & Row, 1989, 11.
[91] Tarnas, Richard, *The Passion of the Western Mind: Understanding the Ideas That Have Shaped Our World Views*, 399.
[92] Allen Ronald J., "Preaching and Postmodernism", 35.
[93] Allen Ronald J., "Preaching and Postmodernism", 36.
[94] Allen Ronald J., "Preaching and Postmodernism", 36
[95] Allen Ronald J., "Preaching and Postmodernism", 37.
[96] Rorty, Richard, "Solidarity or Objectivity?" in Cahoone, Lawrence, ed. *From Modernism to Postmodernism*, 574.
[97] Rorty, Richard, "Solidarity or Objectivity?" in Cahoone, Lawrence, ed. *From Modernism to Postmodernism*, 574.
[98] Anderson, Walter Truett, *Reality Isn't What It Used To Be: Theatrical Politics, Ready-to-Wear Religion, Global Myths, Primitive Chic, and Other Wonders of the Postmodern World*, xii.
[99] Often the "powerful" are identified as Christian, white, European males.
[100] Norris, Christopher, *The Truth About Postmodernism*, Cambridge: Blackwell, 1993, 301.
[101] Anderson, Walter Truett, *Reality Isn't What It Used To Be: Theatrical Politics, Ready-to-Wear Religion, Global Myths, Primitive Chic, and Other Wonders of the Postmodern World*, 183.
[102] Henry, Carl F., "Postmodernism: The New Spectre?" 41.
[103] Oden, Thomas C., "The Death of Modernity and Postmodern Evangelical Spirituality", 24.
[104] Henry, Carl F., "Postmodernism: The New Spectre?" 37.
[105] Henry, Carl F., "Postmodernism: The New Spectre?" 37.
[106] Henry, Carl F. "Postmodernism: The New Spectre?" 37.
[107] Grenz, Stanley J. *A Primer on Postmodernism*, 7.
[108] Oliver, Martyn. *History of Philosophy: Great Thinkers from 600 B.C. to the Present Day*, 173.
[109] Oliver, Martyn. *History of Philosophy: Great Thinkers from 600 B.C. to the Present Day*, 172.
[110] Henry, Carl F. "Postmodernism: The New Spectre?" 42.
[111] Cahoone, Lawrence. *From Modernism to Postmodernism*, 271.
[112] Cahoone, Lawrence, *From Modernism to Postmodernism*.
[113] Adams, Daniel J., "Toward a Theological Understanding of Postmodernism", 526.
[114] Adams, Daniel J., "Toward a Theological Understanding of Postmodernism", 526.
[115] In an essay, Friedrich Nietzsche wrote, "What is truth? A mobile army of metaphors, metonyms and anthropomorphisms—in short, a sum of human relations, which have been enhanced, transposed and embellished poetically and rhetorically, and which after long use seem form, canonical and obligatory to a people: truths are illusions about which one has forgotten that this is what they are;

metaphors which are worn out and without sensuous power; coins which have lost their pictures and now matter only as metal, no longer coins." Nietzsche, Friedrich, "Truth and the Extra-moral Sense", *The Portable Nietzsche*, ed. Walter Kauffmann, New York: Viking, 1968, 46-47.
[116] Grenz, Stanley J., "Star Trek and the Next Generation: Postmodernity and the Future of Evangelical Theology", in *The Challenge of Postmodernism: An Evangelical Engagement*, ed. David S. Dockerty, Wheaton, Ill.: InterVarsity Press, 2001, 113.
[117] Erickson, Millard, *Truth or Consequences: The Promise and Perils of Postmodernism*, Downers Grove, Ill.: InterVarsity Press, 2001, 113.
[118] Grenz, Stanley, "Star Trek and the Next Generation: Postmodernity and the Future of Evangelical Theology", 78.
[119] Erickson, Millard J., *Postmodernizing The Faith: Evangelical Responses to the Challenge of Postmodernism*, 86.
[120] Veith, Gene Edward Jr., *Postmodern Times: A Christian Guide to Contemporary Thought and Culture*, 48.
[121] Grenz, Stanley J., "Star Trek and the Next Generation: Postmodernity and the Future of Evangelical Theology", 79.
[122] Veith, Gene Edward Jr., *Postmodern Times: A Christian Guide to Contemporary Thought and Culture*, 54.
[123] Foucault, Michel. "Nietzsche, Genealogy, History", *Foucault Reader*, ed. Paul Rabinow, New York: Pantheon, 1984, 78-79.
[124] Lyotard, Jean Francois, *The Postmodern Condition: A Report on Knowledge*, xxiii-xxv.
[125] Harvey, David, *The Condition of Postmodernity: An Enquiry into the Origins of Cultural Change*, Cambridge Mass: Blackwell, 1989, 9.
[126] Erickson, Millard J., *Postmodernizing the Faith: Evangelical Responses to the Challenge of Postmodernism*, 110.
[127] Harvey, David, *The Condition of Postmodernity: An Enquiry into the Origins of Cultural Change*, 9.
[128] Harvey, David, *The Condition of Postmodernity: An Enquiry into the Origins of Cultural Change*, 9.
[129] Harvey, David, *The Condition of Postmodernity: An Enquiry into the Origins of Cultural Change*, 9.
[130] Lyotard, Jean Francois, "The Postmodern Condition: A Report on Knowledge" 482. In agreement, Kevin J. Vanhoozer says that Lyotard's definition is, "The best definition of 'postmodern' of which I am aware." Vanhoozer, Kevin J., "Exploring the World; Following the Word: The Credibility of Evangelical Theology in an Incredulous Age," *Trinity Journal*, 16, no. 1, Spring 1995, 3. Any extended discussion of theology's response to postmodernism would be incomplete without reference to: Vanhoozer, Kevin J. (ed.) *The Cambridge Companion to Postmodern Theology*, Cambridge: Cambridge University Press, 2003. There are also two other important works by Vanhoozer which ought to be consulted in this discussion: Vanhoozer, Kevin J., *First Theology: God, Scripture and Hermeneutics*, Leicester: Apollos, 2002 and Vanhoozer, Kevin J., *The Drama of Doctrine*, Louisville: Westminster John Knox Press, 2005.

[131] Tarnas, Richard, *The Passion of the Western Mind: Understanding the Ideas That Have Shaped Our World Views*, 402.

[132] Phillips, Timothy R. and Dennis L. Ockholm, *Christian Apologetics in the Postmodern World*, Downers Grove: InterVarsity Press, 1995, 13.

[133] Veith, Gene Edward Jr., *Postmodern Times: A Christian Guide to Contemporary Thought and Culture*, 53.

[134] Veith, Gene Edward Jr., *Postmodern Times: A Christian Guide to Contemporary Thought and Culture*, 53

[135] Veith, Gene Edward Jr., *Postmodern Times: A Christian Guide to Contemporary Thought and Culture*, 53. It is an interesting argument, but the data could equally support the assertion that human minds tend to organise thought with contrasts in mind, not necessarily to oppress, but merely to understand.

[136] Veith, Gene Edward Jr., *Postmodern Times: A Christian Guide to Contemporary Thought and Culture*, 56.

[137] Erickson, Millard J., *The Postmodern World: Discerning the Times and the Spirit of our Age*, Wheaton, Ill.: Crossway, 2002, 81.

[138] Grenz, Stanley J., "Star Trek and the Next Generation: Postmodernity and the Future of Evangelical Theology", 79.

[139] Rorty, Richard, *Philosophy and the Mirror of Nature*, Princeton N.J.: Princeton University Press, 1979, 176.

[140] Rorty, Richard, *Philosophy and the Mirror of Nature*, 10.

[141] Grenz, Stanley J., *Primer on Postmodernism*, 8.

[142] Grenz, Stanley J., *Primer on Postmodernism*, 8.

[143] Erickson, Millard J., *The Postmodern World: Discerning the Times and the Spirit of our Age*, 52.

[144] Erickson, Millard J., *The Postmodern World: Discerning the Times and the Spirit of our Age*, 52.

[145] Vanhoozer, Kevin J., *Is There a Meaning in This Text?* Grand Rapids: Zondervan, 1998, 19.

[146] Fairlamb, Horace L., *Critical Conditions: Postmodernity and the Questions of Foundations*, 5.

[147] According to Cahoone, Derrida and Foucault are the "two most famous instigators of what is called postmodernism." Cahoone, Lawrence. *From Modernism to Postmodernism*, 336.

[148] Allen, Diognes, "The End of the Modern World," 339.

[149] McGrath, Alister, *Christian Theology*, 114.

[150] Grenz, Stanley J., *A Primer on Postmodernism*, 5-7

[151] Vanhoozer, Kevin J., *Is There a Meaning in This Text?* 20

[152] Anderson, Walter Truett, *Reality Isn't What It Used To Be: Theatrical Politics, Ready-to-Wear Religion, Global Myths, Primitive Chic, and Other Wonders of the Postmodern World*, 90.

[153] Vanhoozer, Kevin J., *Is There a Meaning in This Text?* 53.

[154] Vanhoozer, Kevin J., *Is There a Meaning in This Text?* 53.

[155] McGrath, Alister, *Christian Theology*, 114.

[156] Henry, Carl F., "Postmodernism: The New Spectre?" 36.

[157] Phillips, Timothy R. and Dennis L. Ockholm, *Christian Apologetics in the Postmodern World*, 13.

[158] Tarnas, Richard, *The Passion of the Western Mind: Understanding the Ideas That Have Shaped Our World Views*, 397.

[159] Henry, Carl F., "Postmodernism: The New Spectre?" 41.

[160] D. A. Carson distinguishes empirical or cultural pluralism from philosophical pluralism. Empirical pluralism refers to the growing cultural diversity in our society. Empirical pluralism is a reality and not a philosophical viewpoint. Philosophical pluralism is the belief that all religions are more or less true; no one religion is inherently superior to others. Carson, D. A., *The Gagging of God*, 19.

[161] Oliver, Martyn, *History of Philosophy: Great Thinkers from 600 B.C. to the Present Day*, 173.

[162] Hall, David, "Modern China and the Postmodern West", in Cahoone, L. (ed.) *From Modernism to Postmodernism*, 699.

[163] Anderson, Walter Truett, *Reality Isn't What It Used To Be: Theatrical Politics, Ready-to-Wear Religion, Global Myths, Primitive Chic, and Other Wonders of the Postmodern World*, xi.

[164] Carson, D. A., *The Gagging of God*, 77.

[165] Carson, D. A., *The Gagging of God*, 86.

[166] Allen, Diogenes, "The End of the Modern World", 342.

[167] Allen, Diogenes, "The End of the Modern World", 343.

[168] Rowe, William L., *The Cosmological Argument*, Princeton: Princeton University Press, 1975.

[169] Allen, Diogenes, "The End of the Modern World" 343.

[170] Allen, Diogenes, "The End of the Modern World", 343.

[171] Grenz, Stanley J., *A Primer on Postmodernism*, 2.

[172] Lakeland, Paul, *Postmodernity: Christian Identity in a Fragmented Age*, 13.

[173] Harvey, David, *The Condition of Postmodernity: An Enquiry into the Origins of Cultural Change*, 12-13.

[174] David Lyon suggests the term "postmodern" first came into popular usage after the publication of Jean-Francois Lyotard's, *The Postmodern Condition*. See: Lyon, David, *Postmodernity: Concepts in Social Thought*, 2nd ed. Minneapolis: University of Minnesota Press, 1999, 16.

[175] Lyon. David, *Postmodernity: Concepts in Social Thought*, 16.

[176] Netland, Harold, *Encountering Religious Pluralism: The Challenge to Christian Faith & Mission*, Downers Grove, Ill: InterVarsity, 2001, 59.

[177] Netland, Harold, *Encountering Religious Pluralism: The Challenge to Christian Faith & Mission*, 74.

[178] Netland, Harold, *Encountering Religious Pluralism: The Challenge to Christian Faith & Mission*, 74.

[179] Netland, Harold, *Encountering Religious Pluralism: The Challenge to Christian Faith & Mission*, 85-89.

[180] Oden, Thomas C., *After Modernity...What? Agenda for Theology*, Grand Rapids: Zondervan, 1990, 11. In the preface to this new edition, Oden points out that deconstructionists have adopted the term "ultramodern" instead of postmodern for their work in language. A number of other authors have made similar

arguments suggesting that "postmodernism" is an inaccurate portrayal of the current phenomena. At the other end of the spectrum, there are authors who take the opposite view. Gene Edward Veith adamantly states that "the modern period is over" and postmodernism has arrived. See: Veith, Gene Edward Jr., *Postmodern Times: A Christian Guide to Contemporary Thought and Culture*, Wheaton, Ill.: Crossway, 1994, 19.

[181] Harvey, David, *The Condition of Postmodernity: An Enquiry into the Origins of Cultural Change*, 27.

[182] Grenz, Stanley J., *Primer on Postmodernism*, 4.

[183] Grenz, Stanley J., *Primer on Postmodernism*, 4.

[184] Grenz, Stanley J., *Primer on Postmodernism*, 4.

[185] Erickson, Millard J., *The Postmodern World: Discerning the Times and the Spirit of our Age*, 52.

[186] Veith, Gene Edward Jr., *Postmodern Times: A Christian Guide to Contemporary Thought and Culture*, 38.

[187] Veith, Gene Edward Jr., *Postmodern Times: A Christian Guide to Contemporary Thought and Culture*, 38.

[188] Erickson, Millard J., *The Postmodern World: Discerning the Times and the Spirit of our Age*, 93.

[189] Christians and postmodernists are not necessarily two distinct groups of people as many Christians are influenced by postmodernism and *vice versa*. Just as not all Christians are five-point Calvinists, not all postmoderns subscribe to all the "doctrines" of postmodernism.

[190] Pojman, Louis P., *What Can We Know? An Introduction to the Theory of Knowledge*, xiii.

[191] Many philosophers have observed this critical condition. Foundationalism asserts that a belief is justified if it is self-evident, incorrigible or evident to the senses. But this statement fails to meet its own test. Furthermore, since foundationalism depends on fundamental beliefs upon which other non fundamental beliefs rely, there appears to be an insufficient quantity of basic beliefs to support all other beliefs.

[192] Plantinga, Alvin, *Warranted Christian Belief*, 436.

[193] Erickson, Millard J., *The Postmodern World: Discerning the Times and the Spirit of our Age*, 97.

[194] Derrida, Jacques, *Deconstruction in a Nutshell: A Conversation with Jacques Derrida*, ed. John D. Caputo, New York: Fordham University Press, 1997, 131-132.

[195] Cited earlier as: "what our peers will let us get away with saying" in Rorty, Richard, *Philosophy and the Mirror of Nature*, 176.

[196] Pojman, Louis P., *What Can We Know? An Introduction to the Theory of Knowledge*, 10.

[197] Rorty, Richard., *Philosophy and the Mirror of Nature*, 10.

[198] Plantinga, Alvin, *Warranted Christian Belief*, 430.

[199] This is the view of Stanley Fish and by extension Derrida and Foucault. See: Erickson, Millard J., *The Postmodern World: Discerning the Times and the Spirit of our Age*, 52.

[200] Groothuis, Douglas, *Truth Decay: Defending Christianity Against the Challenges of Postmodernism*, Downers Grove, Ill,: InterVarsity Press, 2000, 94.

[201] Groothuis, Douglas, *Truth Decay:Defending Christianity Against the Challenges of Postmodernism*, 95

[202] Plantinga, Alvin, *Warranted Christian Belief*, 433.

[203] Notwithstanding the fact that the *Genesis* account of creation was one of the Judaic books of the Pentateuch for two millennia prior to the advent of Christianity and continues to be a Judaic sacred text. Plantinga, Alvin, *Warranted Christian Belief*, 436.

[204] Such as the colonial power's version of reality as distinct from the oppressed/colonised perspective. Walter Truett Anderson illustrates the shift in worldview with an imaginary interview with three umpires who explain their philosophy of umpiring: "One says, 'there's balls and there's strikes and I call 'em the way they are.' The second umpire responds, 'there's balls and there's strikes and I call 'em the way I see 'em'. The third says, 'there's balls and there's strikes and they ain't nothin' until I call 'em.'" Anderson explains that the first umpire is objectivist. He operates on the basis of naïve realism. The second umpire is constructivist. He sees the pursuit of truth as something to work towards. The third umpire is a postmodernist. See: Anderson, Walter Truett, *Reality Isn't What It Used To Be: Theatrical Politics, Ready to Wear Religion, Global Myths, Primitive Chic, and Other Wonders of the Postmodern World*, 75.

[205] Lyotard, Jean Francois, *The Postmodern Condition*, xxiii-xxv.

[206] "Culture" here refers primarily to Western culture but postmodernism is growing in global culture as well. The emergence of modernisation, globalisation and urbanisation is bringing the ideas once espoused only in the university campuses to the far reaches of the globe. Certainly there are distinctions that could be made. In some local communities that are less affected by globalisation, these ideas will still remain foreign, but as the world becomes smaller postmodernism will begin to shape those local communities as well. See: Netland, Harold, *Encountering Religious Pluralism: The Challenge to Christian Faith & Mission*, 81-90.

[207] Johnston, Graham, *Preaching to a Postmodern World*, Grand Rapids: IVP, 2001, 15.

[208] Grenz, Stanley J., "Star Trek and the Next Generation: Postmodernism and the Future of Evangelical Theology", 75.

[209] Erickson, Millard J., *The Postmodern World: Discerning the Times and the Spirit of our Age*, 13.

[210] Harvey, David, *The Condition of Postmodernity: An Enquiry into the Origins of Cultural Change*, 38.

[211] Harvey, David, *The Condition of Postmodernity An Enquiry into the Origins of Cultural Change*, 38.

[212] Veith, Gene Edward Jr., *Postmodern Times: A Christian Guide to Contemporary Culture*, 40.

[213] Veith, Gene Edward Jr., *Postmodern Times: A Christian Guide to Contemporary Culture*, 40.

[214] I am not suggesting that *preaching* will be powerless or futile without such knowledge. God has in the past spoken through an ass to correct one of his prophets! Spirit-filled, Christ-centred expository preaching can accomplish God's redemptive and transformative purposes even if the preacher knows nothing about postmodernism.

[215] An inductive approach to expository preaching would be most appropriate in today's culture. This permits hearers of preaching to encounter the Word of God in a manner that allows them to come to a shared ownership of the conclusions, inferences and application of the sermon while remaining faithful to the text of Scripture. This will be examined in chapter three.

CHAPTER THREE: DEVELOPING AN APPROACH TO PREACHING WHICH IS COGNIZANT OF POSTMODERN CULTURE

[1] Capill, Murray A., *Preaching with Spiritual Vigour*, Glasgow: Christian Focus, 2003, 9.

[2] Reymond, Robert L., *The God-Centred Preacher,* Glasgow: Christian Focus, 2003, 13.

[3] Nash, Ronald H., *The Word of God and the Mind of Man*, Phillipsburg: P & R Publishing, 1982, 11.

[4] Kaufman, Gordon D., *God the Problem*, Cambridge: Harvard University Press, 1972, 95.

[5] Stace, W. T., *Mysticism and Human Reason*, University of Arizona Bulletin Series 26, 1955, 19.

[6] Nash, Ronald H., *The Word of God and the Mind of Man*, 12.

[7] Baillie, John, *The Idea of Revelation in Recent Thought, New York*, Columbia University Press, 1956, 29.

[8] Temple, William, *Nature, Man and God*, New York, St Martin's Press, 1934, 316, 322.

[9] Nash, Ronald H., *The Word of God and the Mind of Man*, 13.

[10] Nash, Ronald H., *The Word of God and the Mind of Man*, 14.

[11] Nash, Ronald H., *The Word of God and the Mind of Man*, 29. Epistemological changes in philosophical thinking have been traced earlier. At this point we are concerned to show how those ideas became integrated into theology.

[12] Schleiermacher, Friedrich, *On Religion: Addresses in Response to its Cultural Critics*, Richmond: John Knox Press, 1969, 55.

[13] Schleiermacher, Friedrich, *On Religion: Addresses in Response to its Cultural Critics*, 55-56.

[14] Schleiermacher, Friedrich, *On Religion: Addresses in Response to its Cultural Critics*, 73.

[15] Schleiermacher, Friedrich, *The Christian Faith,* translated from the second German edition, ed. H. R. Mackintosh and J. S. Steward, Edinburgh: T & T Clark, 1928, 260.

[16] Schleiermacher, Friedrich, *The Christian Faith,* 50.

[17] Wells, David F., *God in the Wasteland*, Leicester: Inter-Varsity Press, 1994, 107.

[18] Carson, D. A., *Becoming Conversant with the Emerging Church: Understanding a Movement and Its Implications*, Grand Rapids: Zondervan, 2005, 12. This work is not primarily concerned with the emerging church *per se*, even though one assumes that the emerging church is a peculiarly postmodern phenomenon. Don Carson may be generally cast as an opponent of the emerging church. The work of John Franke is a useful counterbalance to Carson. Franke is particularly interested in engaging postmodern thought and culture from the perspective of Christian faith in order to explore the opportunities and challenges they present for the witness and ministry of the gospel.

[19] Carson, D. A., *Becoming Conversant with the Emerging Church: Understanding a Movement and Its Implications*, 12.

[20] Weber, Gerald K., Available online: <http://www.baptistbulletin.org>. Accessed 7-03-2008.

[21] Weber, Gerald K., Available online: <http://www.baptistbulletin.org>. Accessed 7-03-2008.

[22] Sweet, Leonard, "Theooze". Available online: <http://www.theooze.com>. Accessed 5-3-08; also *Jesus Drives Me Crazy*, Grand Rapids: Zondervan, 2003, 19.

[23] Sweet, Leonard, *Jesus Drives Me Crazy*, Grand Rapids: Zondervan, 2003, 19.

[24] Carson, D. A., Becoming Conversant with the Emerging Church: Understanding a Movement and Its Implications, 14.

[25] Available online: <http://www.emergingchurch.org>. Accessed 6-03-2008.

[26] Mohler, Albert, extract from blog. Available online: <http://www.crosswalk.com/>. Accessed 26-4-2008.

[27] Intelligence and spiritual discernment is not, necessarily, the same thing.

[28] McLaren, Brian, "They Say It's Just A Phase", Next Wave, October 2002, Journal   On-Line,   Available   from   http://http://www.next-wave.org/oct/mclaren2002.htm; Internet, Accessed 5-1-2008.

[29] McLaren, Brian, "They Say It's Just A Phase".

[30] Guinness, Os, *Dining with the Devil*, Grand Rapids: Baker, 1993

[31] 'PastorPete', 2006: Available online: <http://www.opensourcetheology.net/node/856>. Accessed 28-10-2007. The fact that a sermon is confused with a "lecture" is noted.

[32] Doel, Graham, 2006: Available online: <http://www.opensourcetheology.net/node/856>. Accessed 28-10-2007.

[33] Tygrett, Casey, 2006: "Ugly Preaching". Available online: <http://www.theooze.com/article.cmf?id=1193>. Accessed 21-12-2007.

[34] Kimball, Dan, *The Emerging Church: Vintage Christianity for New Generations*, Grand Rapids: Zondervan, 2003, 175.

[35] Capill, Murray A., *Preaching with Spiritual Vigour*, 12.

[36] Lloyd-Jones, Martyn, *Preaching and Preachers*, Grand Rapids: Zondervan, 1971, 91.

[37] Lloyd-Jones, Martyn, *Preaching and Preachers*, 98.

[38] Johnston, Graham, *Preaching to a Postmodern World*, 18.

[39] Leffel, Jim, "Our New Challenge: Postmodernism", *The Death of Truth*, ed. Dennis McCallum, Minneapolis: Bethany House, 1996, 31.

[40] Immink, Gerrit, F., "Homiletics: The Current Debate", *International Journal of Practical Theology*, 2004, 8 (1), 89-121.

[41] Immink, Gerrit, F., "Homiletics: The Current Debate", 89.

[42] Vos, C. J. A., *Theopoetry in the Psalms*, Pretoria: Protea Book House, 2005, 306.

[43] Immink, Gerrit, F., "Homiletics: The Current Debate", 90.

[44] Davis, H. Grady, *Design for Preaching*, Philadelphia: Fortress Press, 1958, 109.

[45] Immink, Gerrit, F., "Homiletics: The Current Debate", 93.

[46] Louw, Johannes P., and Eugene A. Nida, *Greek-English Lexicon of the New Testament*, Bible Society of South Africa, 1989, 412.

[47] Immink, Gerrit, F., "Homiletics: The Current Debate", 93.

[48] Barth, Karl, *The Epistle to the Romans*, trans. from the 6th German edition by Edward C. Hoskyns, New York: Oxford University Press, 1968, 28.

[49] Immink, Gerrit, F., "Homiletics: The Current Debate", 93.

[50] Long, Thomas, *The Witness of Preaching*, Louisville: John Knox Press, 1989, 27.

[51] Immink, Gerrit, F., "Homiletics: The Current Debate", 93.

[52] Bloesch, Donald G. 2001: Available online: <http://www.christianitytoday.com/ct/20001/002/9.54.html>. Accessed 2-10-2007.

[53] Lischer, Richard, *A Theology of Preaching: The Dynamics of the Gospel*, Durham: The Labyrinth Press, 1992, 53.

[54] See: Long, Thomas, *The Witness of Preaching*, Louisville: John Knox Press, 1989.

[55] Bartow, Charles L., *God's Human Speech: A Practical Theology of Proclamation*, Grand Rapids: William B. Eerdmans, 1997, 3.

[56] Bartow, Charles L., *God's Human Speech: A Practical Theology of Proclamation*, 60.

[57] Immink, Gerrit, F., "Homiletics: The Current Debate", 94.

[58] Lindbeck, George, A., *The Nature of Doctrine: Religion and Theology in a Postliberal Age*, Philadelphia: Westminster John Knox, 1984, 33.

[59] Immink, Gerrit, F., "Homiletics: The Current Debate", 95.

[60] Lowry, Eugene, 1997, *The Sermon: Dancing the Edge of Mystery*, Nashville: Abingdon Press, 37.

[61] Immink, Gerrit, F., "Homiletics: The Current Debate", 95.

[62] Bultmann, Rudolph, *Jesus and the Word*, New York: Scribner Press, 1935, 27.

[63] Immink, Gerrit, F., "Homiletics: The Current Debate", 96.

[64] Long, Thomas, *The Witness of Preaching*, 1989, 12.

[65] Immink, Gerrit, F., "Homiletics: The Current Debate", 100.

[66] Craddock, Fred, *As One Without Authority*, Nashville: Abingdon, 1981-62-64.

[67] Lewis, L., and Lewis, G., *Inductive Preaching*, 1983, Illinois: Crossway, 32.

[68] Lewis, L., and Lewis, G., *Learning to Preach Like Jesus*, 1989, Illinois: Crossway, 43.

[69] Immink, Gerrit, F., "Homiletics: The Current Debate", 103.

[70] Rose, Lucy Atkinson, *Sharing the Word: Preaching in the Roundtable Church*, Westminster: John Knox Press, 1997, 4.

[71] Immink, Gerrit, F., "Homiletics: The Current Debate", 104.

[72] Vos, C. J. A., *Theopoetry in the Psalms*, Pretoria: Protea Book House, 2005, 316.

[73] See pp. 9 and 38.

[74] Long, Thomas, *Narrative Structure as Applied to Biblical Preaching*, University Microfilms International, 1980, 64-65.

[75] Vos, C. J. A., "The Rhetorical Mode in Preaching", *Proclaim the Gospel*, ed. C. J. A. Vos, Pretoria: Etiole, 1994, 95.

[76] Davis, H. Grady, *Design for Preaching*, 157.

[77] Long, Thomas, *Preaching and the Literary Form of the Bible*, Philadelphia: Fortress Press, 1989, 71.

[78] Pieterse, H. J. C., *Communicative Preaching*, Pretoria: University of South Africa, 1987, 166. See also Schlafer, D. J., *Surviving the Sermon*, 1992, Cambridge: Cowley Publications, 63, 68-70.

[79] Buttrick, David, *Homiletic Moves and Structures*, Philadelphia: Fortress Press, 1987, 10.

[80] Robinson, W. B., *Journeys Toward Narrative Preaching*, New York: Pilgrim Press, 1990, 34.

[81] Schlafer, D. J., *Surviving the Sermon*, 79.

[82] Long, Thomas, *Preaching and the Literary Form of the Bible*, 75.

[83] Miller, Calvin, "Narrative Preaching", *Handbook of Contemporary Preaching*, ed. Michael Duduit, Nashville: Broadman Press, 1992, 110.

[84] Pieterse, H. J. C., *Communicative Preaching*, 11-17.

[85] Lowry, Eugene L., *The Sermon: Dancing the Edge of Mystery*, 25-27.

[86] Miller, Calvin, "Narrative Preaching", 103.

[87] Miller, Calvin, "Narrative Preaching", 104-106.

[88] Vos, C. J. A., *Theopoetry in the Psalms*, 317.

[89] Rossow, Francis C. "Topical Preaching", *Handbook of Contemporary Preaching*, ed. Michael Duduit, Nashville: Broadman, 1992, 85.

[90] Caemmerer, Richard R., *Preaching for the Church*, St. Louis: Concordia Publishing House, 1959, 133, 139.

[91] Duduit, Michael, ed., *Handbook of Contemporary Preaching*, Nashville: Broadman, 1992, 85.

[92] Allen, Ronald J., *Preaching the Topical Sermon*, Louisville: Westminster John Knox Press, 1992, 3-4.

[93] Broadus, John A., *On the Preparation and Delivery of Sermons*, 4th. ed., revised by Vernon L. Stanfield, San Francisco: Harper & Row, 1979, 55.

[94] Rossow, Francis C. "Topical Preaching", 85.

[95] Rossow, Francis C. "Topical Preaching", 85.

[96] Rossow, Francis C. "Topical Preaching", 85.

[97] Rossow, Francis C. "Topical Preaching", 85.

[98] Broadus, John A., *On the Preparation and Delivery of Sermons*, 55-56.

[99] Rossow, Francis C. "Topical Preaching", 88.

[100] Nehemiah 8:1-8.

[101] Brown, Raymond, *The Message of Nehemiah*, Leicester: Inter-varsity Press, 1998, 127.

[102] Brueggemann, Walter, *An Introduction to the Old Testament: The Canon and Christian Imagination*, Louisville: Westminster John Knox Press, 20003, 367.

[103] Begg, Alistair, *Preaching for God's Glory*, Wheaton: Crossway Books, 1999, 27. See also: Hughes, Jack, *Expository Preaching with Word Pictures*, Ross-shire: Christian Focus, 2001, 19.

[104] Unger, Merril F., *The Principles of Expository Preaching*, Grand Rapids, Illinois: Zondervan, 1955, 33.

[105] Hughes, Jack, *Expository Preaching with Word Pictures*, 69.

[106] Calvin, John, *Institutes of the Christian Religion*, I, trans. Henry Beveridge, Michigan: William B. Eerdmans, 1973, 42.

[107] See: Begg, Alistair, *Preaching for God's Glory*, 28. See also: Robinson, Haddon W., *Biblical Preaching*, Grand Rapids: Baker Book House, 1980, 23.

[108] Hughes, Jack, *Expository Preaching with Word Pictures*, 18.

[109] Available online: <http://www.epcew.org.uk/dpw/DPW.html#preachingoftheword>. Accessed 20-03-2008.

[110] *The Confession of Faith*, The Publications Committee of the Free Presbyterian Church of Scotland, 1970, 379.

[111] Perkins, William, *The Art of Prophesying*, Edinburgh: Banner of Truth, 1996, 9.

[112] Stott, John, *I Believe in Preaching*, London: Hodder and Stoughton, 1982, 125.

[113] Clements, Roy, *The Cambridge Papers*, September, 1998.

[114] Von Rad, G., *Biblical Interpretations in Preaching*, Nashville: Abingdon, 1977, 18.

[115] Buttrick, David, "Interpretation in Preaching" *EA 1*, 1985, 91.

[116] Ebeling, Gerhard, *Theology and Proclamation: A Discussion with Rudolf Bultmann*, trans. by John Riches, London: Collins, 1966, 109.

[117] Logan, Samuel T., "The Phenomenology of Preaching", in Logan, Samuel T., ed., *The Preacher and Preaching: Reviving the Art in the Twentieth Century*, Darlington and Phillipsburg, P and R Publishing Company, 1986, 137.

[118] Stott, John, *Between Two Worlds: The Art of Preaching in the Twentieth Century*, Grand Rapids: William B. Eerdmans, 1982.

[119] Stott, John, *Between Two Worlds: The Art of Preaching in the Twentieth Century*, 190.

[120] Read, David, H. C., *The Communication of the Gospel*, Warrick Lectures, S. C. M., 1952, 62.

[121] Long, Thomas, *The Witness of Preaching*, 12.

[122] Begg, Alistair, *Preaching for God's Glory*, 30.

[123] Vos, C. J. A. *The Rhetorical Mode in Preaching*, 7.

[124] Vos, C. J. A. *The Rhetorical Mode in Preaching*, 7.

[125] Azurdia III, Arturo, *Spirit Empowered Preaching*, Glasgow: Christian Focus, 2003, 29.

[126] Pieterse, H. J. C., *Communicative Preaching*, 15.

[127] Hughes, Jack, *Expository Preaching with Word Pictures*, 85.

[128] Spurgeon, Charles Haddon, *Lectures To My Students*, Grand Rapids: Zondervan, 1970, 127.

[129] Hughes, Jack, *Expository Preaching with Word Pictures*, 85.

[130] Liefeld, W. L., *New Testament Exposition: From Text to Sermon*, Grand Rapids: Zondervan, 1984, 10-13.

[131] Begg, Alistair, *Preaching for God's Glory*, 35.

[132] Stott, John, *Between Two Worlds: The Art of Preaching in the Twentieth Century*, 190.

[133] See Chapell, Bryan, "What is Expository Preaching?", *Journal of Preaching*, 16 (5), 6.

[134] Begg, Alistair, *Preaching for God's Glory*, 33-39.

[135] Owen, John, *The Works of John Owen*, Vol. 16, Edinburgh: Banner of Truth, 1968, 76.

CHAPTER FOUR: INDUCTIVE AND DEDUCTIVE MODES OF PREACHING

[1] Johnston, Graham, *Preaching to a Postmodern World*, 20.

[2] Erickson, Millard J., *Postmodernizing the Faith: Evangelical Responses to the Challenge of Postmodernism*, 151.

[3] Cabal, Ted, "An Introduction of Postmodernity: Where are We, How Did We Get Here, and Can We Get Home?" *The Southern Baptist Journal of Theology*, 5, no. 2, summer 2001, 6.

[4] Middleton, Richard and Brian J. Walsh, *Truth is Stranger than it Used to Be: Biblical Faith in a Postmodern Age*, Downers Grove, Ill.: InterVarsity, 1995, 5.

[5] Mohler, R. Albert Jr., "The Integrity of the Evangelical Tradition and the Challenge of the Postmodern Paradigm", *The Challenge of Postmodernism: An Evangelical Engagement*, 66.

[6] Allen, David L., "Preaching and Postmodernism: An Evangelical Comes to Dance", *The Southern Baptist Journal of Theology*, 5, no. 2, summer, 2001, 64.

[7] Allen, David L., "Preaching and Postmodernism: An Evangelical Comes to Dance", 64.

[8] Erickson, Millard J., *Postmodernizing the Faith: Evangelical Responses to the Challenge of Postmodernism*, 152.

[9] Oden, Thomas C., *After Modernity...What? Agenda for Theology*, 11.

[10] Erickson, Millard J., *Postmodernizing the Faith: Evangelical Responses to the Challenge of Postmodernism*, 153.

[11] *L'Abri* Fellowship began in Switzerland in 1955 when Francis and Edith Schaeffer opened their home to be a place where people might find satisfying answers to their questions and practical demonstration of Christian care. It was called *L'Abri,* the French word for "shelter", because they sought to provide a shelter from the pressures of a relentlessly secular 20th century. As time went by, so many people came that others were called to join the Schaeffer's in their work, and more branches were established in other countries.

[12] Sire, James W., has written a piece detailing this kind of strategy on campuses, entitled, 'Why Should Anyone Believe Anything at All', *Telling the Truth:*

Evangelising Postmoderns, ed. D. A. Carson, Grand Rapids: Zondervan, 2000, 100.

[13] Sweet, Leonard D., *Carpe Manana*, Grand Rapids: Zondervan, 2001, 14.

[14] Sweet, Leonard D., *Postmodern Pilgrims: First Century Passion for the 21st Century World*, Nashville: Broadman & Holman, 2000, xvii.

[15] Sweet, Leonard D., *Postmodern Pilgrims: First Century Passion for the 21st Century World*, xvii.

[16] Sweet, Leonard D., *Carpe Manana*, 68.

[17] Sweet, Leonard D., *Carpe Manana*, 68.

[18] Brian McLaren and Steve Rabey have argued that stories and images that touch the senses cause listeners to be "abducted" by the truth. See: McLaren, Brian, *The Church on the Other Side: Doing Ministry in the Postmodern Matrix*, Grand Rapids: Zondervan, 2000 and: Rabey, Steve, *In Search of Authentic Faith: How Emerging Generations are Transforming the Church*, Colorado Springs: Waterbook Press, 2001. Also: Sweet, Leonard, Brian McLaren and Jerry Haselmayer *'A' is for Abductive: The Language of the Emerging Church*, Grand Rapids: Zondervan, 2003.

[19] Sweet, Leonard D., *Soul Tsunami*, Grand Rapids: Zondervan, 1999, 215.

[20] Mears, Amy and Charles Bugg, "Issues in Preaching in the 21st Century", *Review and Expositor*, 90, no. 1, winter 1993, 341.

[21] Mears, Amy and Charles Bugg, "Issues in Preaching in the 21st Century", 345.

[22] Mears, Amy and Charles Bugg, "Issues in Preaching in the 21st Century", 342.

[23] Scripture affirms that, "there is neither male nor female" (Galatians 3:28) and reflecting this in Scripture itself would be more inclusive.

[24] Kittel's *Theological Dictionary of the New Testament*, Grand Rapids: Eerdmans, 1964, identifies over 30 illustrative words, as does Colin Brown's *New International Dictionary of New Testament Theology*, Grand Rapids: Zondervan, 1967.

[25] The cognate *keryx* is used sometimes in the New Testament (1 Timothy 2:7; 2 Timothy 1:11; 2 Peter 2:5) to describe the preacher as God's royal representative.

[26] Fabarez, Michael, *Preaching that Changes Lives*, Nashville: Thomas Nelson, 2002, 7.

[27] Chapell, Bryan, *Christ-Centred Preaching*, Grand Rapids: Baker Books, 1994. This catalogues the most descriptive terms translated "preaching" and "preachers". See tables 4.1 and 4.2 in that work.

[28] Bauer, Walter, Wilber F., Gingrich, and Frederick W. Danker, *A Greek-English Lexicon of the New Testament and Other Early Christian Literature,* Chicago: University of Chicago Press, 1979, 303.

[29] Eby, David, *Power Preaching for Church Growth*, Mentor, 1998.

[30] Many publishers reprint works on preaching (e.g. Banner of Truth Trust). But many authors refer to preachers of a previous time to uphold the value of preaching today.

[31] Sangster, William E., *The Craft of Sermon Construction*, reprint, Grand Rapids: Baker Book House, 1972, 187.

[32] Sangster, William E., *The Craft of Sermon Construction*, 25-26.

[33] Sangster, William E., *The Craft of Sermon Construction*, 25-26.

[34] Calvin, John. In: Miller, Graham, *Calvin's Wisdom*, Edinburgh: Banner of Truth, 1992, 252.

[35] Bonhoeffer, Deitrich, *Worldly Preaching: Lectures on Homiletics*, trans. Clyde E. Fant, Nashville: Thomas Nelson, 1975, 145.

[36] Hilborn, David, In: Clements, Roy. "Expository Preaching in a Postmodern World", *Evangelical Review of Theology* 23, no. 2, April 1999, 174.

[37] Bartel, Don, "Evangelising Postmoderns", *Telling the Truth: Evangelizing Postmoderns*, ed. D. A. Carson, Grand Rapids: Zondervan, 2000, 343.

[38] Long, Jimmy, "Generating Hope: A Strategy for Reaching the Postmodern Generation", *Telling the Truth: Evangelizing Postmoderns*, 328.

[39] Azurdia, Arturo, *Spirit Empowered Preaching: The Vitality of the Holy Spirit in Preaching,* U.K.: Christian Focus, 1998, 30.

[40] Azurdia is particularly critical of some of the church growth models.

[41] Keller, Tim, "Preaching Morality in an Amoral Age", *Leadership* 17, winter, 1996, 112-115.

[42] Keller, Tim, "Preaching Morality in an Amoral Age", 114

[43] Keller, Tim, Preaching Morality in an Amoral Age', 115.

[44] Broadus, John A., *On the Preparation and Delivery of Sermons*, 54-60.

[45] 2 Timothy 3:16

[46] Exegesis is used also to describe the elucidation of philosophical and legal texts. Although the most widely-known exegeses concern themselves with Christian, Jewish and Islamic books, analyses also exist of books of other religions.

[47] See: Fee, Gordon D., *New Testament Exegesis,* Louisville, KY.: Westminster/John Knox Press, revised edition, 1993.

[48] In the field of biblical exegesis scholars take great care to avoid eisegesis. In this field, eisegesis is regarded as "poor exegesis". While some denominations and scholars denounce biblical eisegesis, many Christians are known to employ it-albeit inadvertently-as part of their own experiential theology. Modern evangelical scholars accuse liberal Protestants of practicing biblical eisegesis, while mainline scholars accuse fundamentalists of practicing eisegesis. Catholics say that all Protestants engage in eisegesis, because the bible can be correctly understood only through the lens of Holy Tradition as handed down by the institutional Church. Jews counter that all Christians practice eisegesis when they read the Hebrew Bible as a book about Jesus.

[49] Robinson, Haddon W., *Biblical Preaching: The Development and Delivery of Expository Messages*, Grand Rapids: Baker, 1980, 20.

[50] Robinson, Haddon W., *Biblical Preaching: The Development and Delivery of Expository Messages*, 21.

[51] Robinson, Haddon W., *Biblical Preaching: The Development and Delivery of Expository Messages*, 24.

[52] See pp. 44-45

[53] Stott, John R. W., *Between Two Worlds: The Art of Preaching in the 20th Century*, Grand Rapids: Eerdmans, 1982, 138.

[54] Clements, Roy, "Expository Preaching in a Postmodern World", 178-179.

[55] Piper, John, "The Divine Majesty of the Word: John Calvin, The Man and His Preaching", *Southern Baptist Journal of Theology* 3, no. 2, summer 1999, 13.

56 Piper, John, "The Divine Majesty of the Word: John Calvin, The Man and His Preaching", 13-14.

57 Carson, D. A., "Six Reasons Not to Abandon Expository Preaching", *Leadership* 17, summer 1996, 87-88.

58 Swank, J. Grant Jr., "Excitement About Expository Preaching", *Preaching* 6, no. 1, July-August 1990, 9.

59 Murray, Ian H. D., *Martyn Lloyd-Jones: The Fight of Faith 1939-1961*, Edinburgh: Banner of Truth, 1990, 261.

60 Mayhue, Richard L., "Rediscovering Expository Preaching", *Rediscovering Expository Preaching*, ed. Richard L. Mayhue, Dallas: Word, 1992, 12.

61 Hilborn, David, *Picking Up the Pieces: Can Evangelicals Adapt to Contemporary Culture?* London: Hodder and Stoughton, 1997.

62 Clements, Roy, "Expository Preaching in a Postmodern World", 175-176.

63 This is expressly stated in relation to the Johanine literature (1 John 1:1) but is equally true of all Scripture authors.

64 Clements, Roy, "Expository Preaching in a Postmodern World", 177.

65 Larsen, C. F. David, *The Company of Preachers: A History of Biblical Preaching from the Old Testament to the Modern Era*, Grand Rapids: Kregel, 1998, 27-30.

66 Clements, Roy, "Expository Preaching in a Postmodern World", 178.

67 Allen, David L., "A Tale of Two Roads: The New Homiletic and Biblical Authority", *Preaching* 18, Sept-Oct., 36.

68 Heflin, James and Millard Erickson, *Old Wine in New Wineskins: Doctrinal Preaching in a Changing World*, Grand Rapids: Baker Books, 1997, 167-82. Heflin shows the variety of views concerning the meaning of "expository preaching" in his review of popular preachers.

69 Greidanus, Sidney, *The Modern Preacher and the Ancient Text: Interpreting and Preaching Biblical Literature*, Grand Rapids: Eerdmans, and Leicester: Inter-Varsity Press 1988 (reprinted 1996).

70 As cited by Bernard Ramm in *Protestant Biblical Interpretation: A Textbook of Hermeneutics* 3rd. ed., Grand Rapids: Baker Book House, 1970, xiv.

71 Vos, A., "Scholasticism", *New Dictionary of Theology,* eds. Sinclair B. Ferguson and David F. Wright, Downers Grove: InterVarsity Press, 2000, 622.

72 Dargan, Edwin Charles, *A History of Preaching*, Grand Rapids: Baker Book House, 1954, vol. 1, 232.

73 Dargan is careful to point out exceptions like Gilbert Voetius who were "scholastic in type and uncompromising in Spirit...along with his scholasticism and dogmatism he carried a very genuine piety." Dargan, Edwin Charles, *A History of Preaching*, vol. 2, 79.

74 Somerville, Jim, "Preaching to the Right Brain", *Preaching* 10, no. 4, Jan-Feb, 1995, 36.

75 Somerville, Jim, "Preaching to the Right Brain", 36.

76 Sweet, Leonard D., *Postmodern Pilgrims: First Century Passion for the 21st Century World*, xxi.

77 Brian McLaren and Steve Rabey have argued for a third approach they call "abduction" which involves using a story that touches the senses in such a way that

listeners are abducted by the truth. See: McLaren, Brian, *The Church on the Other Side: Doing Ministry in the Postmodern Matrix*. See also: Rabey, Steve, *In Search of Authentic Faith: How Emerging Generations are Transforming the Church*.
[78] Robinson, Haddon W., Biblical *Preaching: The Development and Delivery of Expository Messages*, 125-127. See also: Allen, David, *A Tale of Two Roads: The New Homiletic and Biblical Authority*, 36.
[79] Craddock, Fred B., *As One Without Authority*, Nashville: Parthenon Press, 1971, 10. There is much in Craddock's treatment of inductive preaching that is helpful; however, some of his hermeneutical inclinations are questionable. Some have taken the view that Craddock rejects the authority of Scripture and there may be some warrant for reading him that way. It can be maintained that Scripture is already authoritative, but the methodology we use to proclaim it may in fact help those who reject its authority to ultimately accept its authority and believe it.
[80] The average person in the pew probably misses his remote control when the sermon becomes dry.
[81] Craddock, Fred B., *As One Without Authority*, 63.
[82] Lewis, Ralph L. and Gregg Lewis, *Inductive Preaching: Helping People Listen*, Westchester, Ill.: Crossway Books, 1983, 36.
[83] Spurgeon, Charles Haddon, *Lectures to My Students*, Grand Rapids: Zondervan, 1954, 349.
[84] Lewis, Ralph L. and Gregg Lewis, *Inductive Preaching: Helping People Listen*, 43.
[85] Lewis, Ralph L. and Gregg Lewis, *Inductive Preaching: Helping People Listen*, 45.
[86] Lewis, Ralph L. and Gregg Lewis, *Inductive Preaching: Helping People Listen*, 165.
[87] Lewis, Ralph L. and Gregg Lewis, *Inductive Preaching: Helping People Listen*, 119.
[88] Lewis, Ralph L. and Gregg Lewis, *Inductive Preaching: Helping People Listen*, 119.
[89] Lewis, Ralph L. and Gregg Lewis, *Inductive Preaching: Helping People Listen*, 119.
[90] Lewis, Ralph L. and Gregg Lewis, *Inductive Preaching: Helping People Listen*, 119.
[91] Middleton, Richard and Brian J. Walsh, *Truth is Stranger than it Used to Be: Biblical Faith in a Postmodern Age*, 83. Middleton and Walsh point out that the Bible is the "ultimate metanarrative", but the biblical metanarrative is different from other metanarratives. The biblical metanarrative seeks to show a way out of suffering and disenfranchisement; it seeks to invite others into its story rather than exclude them.
[92] Lewis, Ralph L. and Gregg Lewis, *Inductive Preaching: Helping People Listen*, 119.
[93] Lewis, Ralph L. and Gregg Lewis, *Inductive Preaching: Helping People Listen*, Lewis and Lewis, 119.
[94] Lewis, Ralph L. and Gregg Lewis, *Inductive Preaching: Helping People Listen*, Lewis and Lewis, 119.

[95] Lewis, Ralph L. and Gregg Lewis, *Inductive Preaching: Helping People Listen*, Lewis and Lewis, 119.

[96] Lewis, Ralph L. and Gregg Lewis, *Inductive Preaching: Helping People Listen*, Lewis and Lewis, 61.

[97] Robinson, Haddon W., *Biblical Preaching: The Development and Delivery of Expository Messages*, 125-127.

[98] Broadus, John A., *On the Preparation and Delivery of Sermons*, 4th ed. rev. Vernon L. Stanfield, 149.

[99] Robinson, Haddon W., *Biblical Preaching: The Development and Delivery of Expository Messages*, 68-74.

[100] Larsen, David L., *Telling the Old, Old Story, The Art of Narrative Preaching*, Kregel Academic and Professional, 2001, 22.

[101] Lowry, Eugene L., *The Homiletical Plot: the Sermon as Narrative Art Form*, Atlanta: John Knox Press, 1980, 15.

[102] Lowry, Eugene L., *The Homiletical Plot: the Sermon as Narrative Art Form*, 21.

[103] Lowry, Eugene L., *The Homiletical Plot: the Sermon as Narrative Art Form*, 25.

[104] Lowry, Eugene L., *The Homiletical Plot: the Sermon as Narrative Art Form*, 30.

[105] Lowry, Eugene L., *The Homiletical Plot: the Sermon as Narrative Art Form*, 56.

[106] Lowry, Eugene L., *The Homiletical Plot: the Sermon as Narrative Art Form*, 61.

[107] Lowry, Eugene L., *The Homiletical Plot: the Sermon as Narrative Art Form*, 71.

[108] Lowry, Eugene L., *The Homiletical Plot: the Sermon as Narrative Art Form*, 85.

[109] Lowry, Eugene L., *The Sermon: Dancing the Edge of Mystery*, 57.

[110] Adams, J. E., *Preaching with Purpose*, Grand Rapids: Baker, 1982, 93.

[111] Lowry, Eugene L., "The Revolution of Sermonic Shape", *Listening to the Word* (In Honor of Fred B. Craddock) ed. Gail R. O' Day & Thomas G. Long, Abingdon Press, 1993, 99.

[112] Adams, J. E., *Preaching with Purpose*, 156-157.

[113] In Matthew 11:1, 1Timothy 5:17; 6:2, and Acts15:35; 28:31, they are used in the same sentence "preaching and teaching". In the Acts 28:31 f. passage, Luke writes that Paul was, "proclaiming the kingdom of God and teaching about the Lord Jesus Christ..." This may point to some distinction between the two terms in Luke's mind.

[114] The word "teaching" and its cognates occurs twice as often as "preaching". The word διδάσκω (didásko) and cognates occurs 179 times in the New Testament and the words like κηρύσσω (kerússo) and ευαγγελλίζω (euaggellízo) occur 83 times.

[115] Lawson, Steven J., "Sola Scriptura: The Sufficiency of Scripture in Expository Preaching", *Preaching* 18, no. 2, Sept.-Oct. 2002, 20-26. I will be following Lawson's article closely and utilising the texts he references in his article in this discussion.

[116] Adams, J. E., *Preaching with Purpose*, xi.

[117] Robinson, Haddon W., *Biblical Preaching: The Development and Delivery of Expository Messages*, 34

[118] Eslinger, Richard L., The *Web of Preaching*, Nashville: Abingdon Press, 2002, 201.

[119] Mears, Amy and Charles Bugg, 'Issues in Preaching in the 21st Century', *Review and Expositor* 90, no. 1, winter 1993, 341.

[120] Adams, J. E., *Preaching with Purpose*, 156-157.

[121] Pitt-Watson, Ian, Cited in: Greidanus, Sidney. *The Modern Preacher and the Ancient Text: Interpreting and Preaching Biblical Literature*, 184-185.

[122] McCullough, Donald W., *The Trivialization of God: The Dangerous Illusion of A Manageable Deity*, Colorado Springs: Nav Press, 1995, 32.

[123] Augustine, Aurelius (Saint), *On Christian Doctrine*, 4.27.59.

[124] Dallimore, Arnold, *George Whitfield, The Life and Times of the Great Evangelist of the 18th Century Revival*, Banner of Truth Trust, 1980, vol. 1, 116-117.

[125] Sanders, Oswald, *Men in God's School*, London: Marshall, Morgan and Scott, no date, 174.

[126] Robinson, Haddon, "What Authority Do We Have Anymore?" in: Robinson, Haddon and Craig Brian Larson, eds. *The Art & Craft of Biblical Preaching: A Comprehensive Resource for Today's Communicators*, Zondervan, 2005, 26.

[127] MacArthur, John, "Foreword", in: Fabarez, Michael. *Preaching That Changes Lives*, vii.

[128] With regard to the absence of any mention of "persuading" or "explaining" in Berea it is known that he travelled to Berea and that on arrival entered the synagogue. The Bereans received the message more readily (this is clear from the text), although they did search the Scriptures to see if what Paul said was true. This probably accounts for the fact that there is no mention of "persuading" or "explaining" in Berea.

[129] See Acts 17:10-12.

[130] "For they say, 'His letters are weighty and strong, but his bodily presence is weak, and his speech of no account.'" (2 Corinthians 10:10).

[131] Paul was perceived by some to be an inadequate public speaker but in reality he was a powerful orator. Nevertheless he did not depend merely on his own skill to bring about conviction and conversion. The word "hearts" was understood to refer to the mind, emotions and will. See 1 Corinthians 2:1-4.

[132] Dabney, Robert L, *Evangelical Eloquence: A Course of Lectures on Preaching*, Banner of Truth Trust, 1999, 260.

[133] Calvin, John, *Commentaries on the Epistles of Paul the Apostle to the Romans*, Edinburgh: Calvin Translation Society, 1849, 400-401.

[134] Spurgeon, Charles Haddon, *Lectures to my Students*, reprinted ed., Pasadena: Pilgrim Publications, 1990, 96.

[135] Sargent, Tony, *The Sacred Anointing*, Wheaton: Crossway Books, 1994, 29.

[136] From the Greek, to incite:- persuade (anapeithō) Fernando, Ajith, "The Uniqueness of Jesus Christ", in: Carson, D. A. ed. *Telling the Truth:Evangelising Postmoderns*, Grand Rapids: Zondervan, 2000, 126.

[137] Fernando, Ajith, "The Uniqueness of Jesus Christ", 127.

[138] Fernando, Ajith, "The Uniqueness of Jesus Christ", 127.

[139] Fernando, Ajith, "The Uniqueness of Jesus Christ", 127.

[140] Calvin, John, *Gen. Epp.* 369.

[141] *Acts* 17:1-4

[142] *Acts* 18:18-19

[143] Carson, D. A., The *Primacy of Expository Preaching*, cassette.

[144] "Come now, let us *reason* together, says the Lord: though your sins are like scarlet, they shall be as white as snow; though they are red like crimson, they shall become like wool." (Isaiah 1:18 emphasis added in italicisation).
[145] MacArthur, John Jr., "Foreword" to Fabarez, Michael. *Preaching That Changes Lives*, vii.
[146] Phillips, Timothy and Denis. L. Okholm, *Christian Apologetics in a Postmodern World*, Downers Grove, Illinois: InterVarsity Press, 1995, 19.
[147] Tozer, Aiden Wilson, *The Best of A. W, Tozer*, comp. Warren W. Wiersbe, Grand Rapids: Baker Book House, 1978, 140-141.
[148] Packer, James Innell in: Lucas, Dick et. al. *Preaching the Living Word: Addresses from the Evangelical Ministry Assembly*, Great Britain: Christian Focus Publications, 1999, 31.
[149] Broadus, John A., *On the Preparation and Delivery of Sermons*, 4th. ed., revised by Vernon L. Stanfield, 165.
[150] Broadus, John A., *On the Preparation and Delivery of Sermons*, revised by Vernon L. Stanfield, 165.
[151] McGrath, Alister, *Bridge-Building: Effective Christian Apologetics*, Leicester, England: IVP, 1992, 81.
[152] Johnston, Graham, *Preaching To A Postmodern World*, Leicester: Inter-Varsity Press, 2001, 108.
[153] Some T.V. evangelists in the, particularly in the USA.
[154] Lucas, Dick, (ed. et. al.) *Preaching the Living Word: Addresses from the Evangelical Ministry Assembly*, 31.
[155] Although he did not reject Nicodemus Jesus rebuked him for his ignorance of spiritual matters and classified him as part of a group blinded by prejudice rather than receptive to the New Covenant.
[156] Middleton, Richard and Brian J. Walsh, *Truth is Stranger than it Used to Be: Biblical Faith in a Postmodern Age*, 105.
[157] Kaiser, Walter C. Jr., *Toward an Exegetical Theology: Biblical Exegesis for Preaching and Teaching,* Grand Rapids: Baker Book House, 1981, (twelfth printing 1996). Kaiser is quoting John Albert Bengel, *Gnomon of the New Testament*, ed. Andrew R. Fausset, 5 Vols., Edinburgh: Clark, 1857-1858, 1:7. He notes that the English translation has been modernised at one or two points.
[158] Kaiser, Walter C. Jr., *Toward an Exegetical Theology: Biblical Exegesis for Preaching And Teaching*, 7.
[159] Piper, John, *The Supremacy of God in Preaching*, Grand Rapids: Baker House Books, 1990, 40.
[160] Murray, Andrew, *Humility*, New Kensington: Pa.: Whitaker House, 1982, 19.
[161] Acts 17:32.
[162] Flavel, John, *The Works of John Flavel*, Reprinted, Banner of Truth Trust, 1968, Vol. 6, 562.
[163] Piper, John, *The Supremacy of God in Preaching*, 33.
[164] Migliore, Daniel L., *Faith Seeking Understanding: An Introduction to Christian Theology*, Grand Rapids: Michigan, Eerdmans, 1991.
[165] Johnston, Graham, *Preaching to a Postmodern World*, 105.

[166] Cited by Stewart, James S., *Heralds of God: A Practical Book on Preaching*, Regent College Publishing, 1946, 210.

[167] Stewart, James S., *Heralds of God: A Practical Book on Preaching*, 212

[168] Norrington, David C., *To Preach Or Not To Preach: The Church's Urgent Question*, Carlisle, Cumbria: Paternoster, 1996, 1.

[169] Sewall, Gilbert T., "The Postmodern Schoolhouse", *Dumbing Down: Essays on the Strip-Mining of American Culture*, Katherine Washbourn and John Thornton (eds.), New York & London: W. W. Norton & Company, 65-66.

INDEX